MY LIFE
as a
MIRACLE

MY LIFE as a MIRACLE

The Wizard

CANTERBURY UNIVERSITY PRESS

For Alice,
for hanging in there

First published in 1998 by
CANTERBURY UNIVERSITY PRESS
Private Bag 4800, Christchurch, New Zealand

Copyright © 1998 The Wizard
Copyright © 1998 Canterbury University Press

ISBN 0-908812-73-6

This book is copyright. Except for the purpose of fair review,
no part may be stored or transmitted in any form or by any means,
electronic or mechanical, including recording or storage in
any information-retrieval system, without permission in writing
from the publishers. No reproduction may be made, whether by
photocopying or by any other means, unless a licence has been
obtained from the publisher or its agent.

Cover photograph by Kurt Langer
Designed and typeset at Canterbury University Press
Printed by Rainbow Print, Christchurch

contents

1
A child at war

I came into the world in Battersea, London, at ten past one in the afternoon on Sunday, 4 December in the year 1932, according to Christian reckoning.

I was never able to convince my mother how important my birth was and how fortunate she should consider herself to be the vehicle I had chosen for my incarnation. No doubt, in the future, all sorts of myths will arise involving angels, earthquakes, eclipses and other spectacular signs. These always go down well with simple folk who cannot appreciate subtler signs of uniqueness. I have a statistical proof that, far from being random, the time and place of my birth were magically preordained, at a chance of 36,000 to 1!

My mother, Emy, and my father, Arthur, had met while teaching together and after a long wait – married women were not allowed to be teachers at that time – had left their humble rural backgrounds in East Anglia to work in the slums of London. But they returned to Framlingham, my mother's family home, with their wonderful baby, to have me baptised Ian Brackenbury Channell at St Michael's on Easter Day 1933.

The first two years of my life were spent mainly on all fours, since I found that I could move at remarkable speed in that position and was reluctant to give up a tried and tested method of locomotion for a risky novelty such as walking. This was an early indication of both my extreme conservatism and my strong affinity with the animals.

I found civilisation distasteful and would escape from parental control the moment I was not being observed and at this time, and for a year or two afterwards, I was forcibly restrained by being tied in my walker or imprisoned in a wooden cage with a net over the top, from which I made a series of courageous but unsuccessful escape bids. When not thus tied down I was put on a leash and taken for walks. I was occasionally allowed to race freely about in Clapham Park, stealing other children's footballs and the like.

During this period I developed strong feelings of self-importance, as I was the centre of my parents' world and found them a willing audience to my early crude attempts at spellbinding. I was assured by my mother that

My parents, Emy and Arthur, in the mid-1920s.

My baptismal certificate.

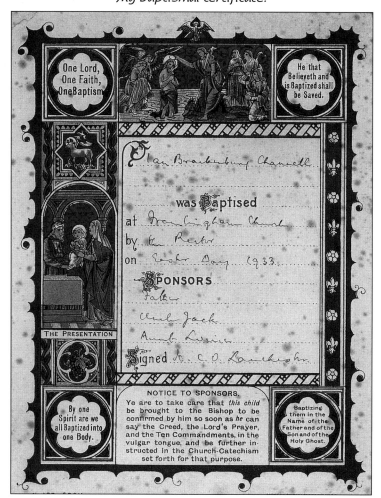

One Lord, One Faith, One Baptism

He that Believeth and is Baptized shall be Saved.

THE PRESENTATION

Ian Brackenbury Channell

was Baptised

at Framlingham Church

by the Rector

on Easter Day 1933

SPONSORS

Father

Uncle Jack

Aunt Lizzie

Signed A. C. O. Lanchester

NOTICE TO SPONSORS.

Ye are to take care that *this child* be brought to the Bishop to be confirmed by him so soon as *he* can say the Creed, the Lord's Prayer, and the Ten Commandments, in the vulgar tongue, and be further instructed in the Church-Catechism set forth for that purpose.

By one Spirit are we all Baptized into one Body.

Baptizing them in the Name of the Father and of the Son and of the Holy Ghost.

I danced continuously once I was persuaded to give up the beastly method of movement I preferred. Moreover, I never cried or woke my parents from their slumbers.

Paradise lost

This blissful state was suddenly shattered one memorable day – 14 January 1935, to be precise – when my father took me upstairs to see my mother, who had not been well. Her memory of that occasion was still crystal clear (over fifty years later), so profound was the shock in my face when I saw another in the arms of the one I thought was mine alone.

Aged seven months, with my father in London.

Having chosen the Sabbath to appear in the world, I was the proverbial 'blithe and bonny, good and gay' child. I was indeed so beautiful with my gold curls, twinkling eyes and angelic smile that old ladies would stop my mother to tell her what a beautiful little girl she had.

I had a sister, Hilary. A usurper of my rightful place. A rival for my deity's affections. A distraction from the real issue . . . me!

She was a plump child with an unpleasant disposition and cried for attention, which she could not win by personal charm and a sunny disposition like my own. As the years went by, she improved considerably in appearance. She became a professor of sociology and a champion of all those people who use similar techniques to get what they want.

Through the evil power of jealousy, I was suddenly transformed from a happy, confident child into a vile, anxiety-ridden monster. I directed many unkind acts of hostility towards my sister, such as shaking her pram until she cried or pinching her when no one was looking. To allay my agony, my mother bought me a soft little kitten but as I attempted to strangle it and swung it round by its tail, she got rid of it before I did. This jealousy, of course, is a thing of the past.

Ritual humiliation

Shortly after the appearance of my rival I experienced another traumatic shock, a foretaste of others to follow. My father took me away one day and, to my mother's horror, I was shorn of my beautiful golden curls and my hair was slicked down with hair cream.

For the next thirty-three years I was forced to endure this monthly humiliation, yet another case of discrimination against men. It was not until 1968 that I managed to put my foot down and I am proud to say that I have not had a haircut since. I believe that, apart from some miserable anti-social hermits, I hold the record for barbarism in Australasia.

The day of the first haircut.

My first love

Towards the end of 1934 we had moved into a new semi-detached in Petts Wood in North Kent on the fringe of suburban London. Soon, however, a serpent entered my narcissistic private paradise . . . once again in the form of a woman!

Next door lived a beautiful young girl a couple of years older than me and, aged three, I felt the first tug at my heartstrings. This was the beginning of an affair that lasted until September 1939, when we were cruelly parted by the evacuation plans of the Second World War, never to be reunited. Many years later I learnt that she named her first son Ian. Like one of my heroes, Hector Berlioz, I think I may have been permanently marked by this unfulfilled infantile passion: perhaps, as with the composer, the impression left upon me by this gentle and charming girl may grow stronger as the years go by.

It is at this time that I begin to have memories of my own and can supplement information my mother later supplied regarding my infancy. Children live in a world of giants and all the furniture appears monstrously clumsy and alien. I can remember my delight in being given a chair made especially for me by my father. It was really special and its shiny orange-yellow colour was another source of delight. Even more thrilling was the present given to me that year by a benevolent deity known as Father Christmas, a bright red pedal-car with running boards supporting a small petrol can and with its own side mirror.

In April 1936 my father took a snapshot that captures my character at the age of three – intelligent, cautious and looking for mischief.

The hideous vortex

These years were not all unalloyed pleasure, of course. Apart from the sibling rivalry there was the dreaded plughole. This was my first and only phobia. Being a water baby (The Water Babies was my favourite tale as a child), I would jump and splash about in the bath and steadfastly refuse to get out, no matter what the reward offered or the punishment threatened.

One day, by sheer chance, during my mother's Herculean struggle to extract me, the plug was inadvertently pulled out while I was still in the bath. My face went pale and I stiffened with fear at the sight of the hideous vortex with its accompanying sucking noise. I leapt out in a flash. There was no more difficulty in persuading me that bath time was over.

I still have a morbid fear of vortices that suck things down and since autobiographies are supposed to be full of juicy titbits for the noseyparker readers I confess that I still get well out of the bath once the plug is pulled out and the sucking noise starts.

Early promise

I badgered my mother, who was a trained primary schoolteacher, to allow me to attend the local prep school, St Dunstan's. I was very happy there and can remember being given a shiny new penny for learning how to tie my shoelaces. My mother informed me that I was extremely popular with the teachers.

In primitive societies those destined to become medicine men, witch-doctors, shamans or wizards will start as infants to imitate animals and to perform before large numbers of adults without embarrassment. I can now see that my destiny was marked out for me at St Dunstan's, and my spectacularly unsuccessful struggles to avoid it by trying to fit in with people who held to rigid secular or religious ideologies will provide much of the material for the first half of my life story.

It was at St Dunstan's School that I was first encouraged to appear on the stage. My performance of A. A. Milne's 'John's got great big waterproof boots on' was a great success, but in my own heart my bunny costume, again preserved by a fortunate photograph, was the highlight of my early days as a performer.

End of an era

The period between the First and Second World Wars has a flavour all of its own; to taste it, read Winnie the Pooh, The Wind in the Willows and Just William. That fine summer of 1939 brings back memories of trips to the London Zoo at Regents Park, washing Jet, our black cocker spaniel, playing with my pet tortoise and a trip to Felixstowe for all the fun of the seaside.

There were hints of a different world just around the corner. When I went down to the shops to buy a packet of gum with a mystery gift for a farthing, I used to stop and watch the new television programmes in the shop window. I also had a model of the world's fastest aircraft, the Supermarine Spitfire, and I wanted to fly.

A visit to the seaside of Lowestoft in August 1937 is typical of a life-long lover of messing about on the beach with bucket and spade. Here my father is instructing my sister and me in the art. In the pool is my red tin-hulled yacht, still fresh in my memory though it perished sixty years ago. My passion for building sandcastles is so great that I have continued to build them when all others have grown out of such foolish enterprises.

Seaside fun, August 1938.

The day war broke out

I remember the awed silence as we sat around the radio set and listened to Neville Chamberlain's quiet voice declaring war on Nazi Germany and the tremendous rumpus of the issuing of gas masks. My sister, being only four at the time, had an attractive Mickey Mouse gas mask whereas mine was just a smaller version of the adult mask. I was extremely envious.

I left my school in Petts Wood and went up to London each day with my father to Albany Road School, where he taught. After a week or two my sister and I were suddenly put on a train with our gas masks in square cardboard boxes around our necks, labels pinned on us showing our names and address, and a tin of corned beef each. We were sent to Weymouth, a fishing and seaside town in Dorset; we were 'evacuees'.

At first we were lonely and rather lost in our new surroundings, though I had already made quite a long train journey on my own from Petts Wood to my grandparents' place at Framlingham in Suffolk. My father and mother soon joined us and we got a pleasant house near Radipole Lake in the town.

Dorset is a most beautiful county and I came to be spellbound by the chalk downs, Iron Age burial mounds, sea cliffs, medieval ruins and strange monsters etched out in the limestone hills thousands of years ago. With our father we walked enormous distances for young children. There was a beautiful sandy beach for making sandcastles, the fishing harbour was intensely interesting, the rock pools were full of strange creatures and nearby were the ruins of an old castle. Huge battleships were anchored at Portland, a mile or two along the coast, and there was a pier full of fascinating slot machines.

I was not able at the time to make a tactical analysis of the wisdom of evacuating London schoolchildren to the nearest port to the Channel Islands and a few miles away from one of the main south coast bases of the British Navy. As a seven-year-old I was excited rather than scared when some of the earliest air raids over England took place above Weymouth.

I can remember one day seeing hundreds of French soldiers lying around the town, in shabby uniforms, without rifles or packs. My parents took some in for meals and baths, since they were in a state of shock and had no idea what to do. They were the remains of the French regular army who had been hurriedly sent to the south coast after they were rescued from Dunkirk. Then, after a few days, they were gone. I was told later that they had all gone back to France to surrender!

Shortly afterwards the whole town turned out to see the arrival of refugees from the Channel Islands. The atmosphere was extremely tense and even I could feel the desperation behind the cheerful singing of 'Run, Rabbit, Run' and 'There'll Always Be an England'.

The summer of 1940 was beautiful and we spent a lot of time on the beach. I was irresistibly drawn to the Punch and Judy show and watched the ancient traditional drama over and over again. The essential part played by the crowd; the highly abstract and dynamic presentation of Punch-Adam and Judy-Eve; Punch's solo stand against the world of wife, baby, monster, ghost, bureaucrat and policeman, all out to spoil his fun – this appealed to the masculine side of my developing personality.

Then, in the autumn, the pier closed down, the donkeys, the sand sculptors and the Punch and Judy man disappeared forever. The beach was sealed off by barbed wire. The last remnants of the pre-war days were gone, only to live in the minds of those who knew them.

The war in inner space

Up till now my story has dwelt on the pretty dramatic outer events that moulded my first few years. Of equal importance to all of us are the events in our inner worlds, and it is slowly being realised that we spend a third of our lives sleeping, not to rest our bodies but to develop our personalities. I don't know when the nightmares started, but I can date them to shortly before the war at the latest. During the years that followed I was far more terrified of my own imagination when dreaming than I was of being injured or killed by traffic or German bombers. It was not pain or death that frightened me but something much worse. I would begin to think that there might be something horrible in the cupboard or in the chest of drawers or behind the curtain. No sooner had I thought there might be, than there was! As with all paranoia, I had produced the very situation that I feared.

Slowly, however, I began to gain control of these hideous nightmares that left me sweating with fear. I learnt to pinch myself and wake up. This was possible only by immense efforts of concentration in which I experimented with reality. I would say to myself, 'I don't know if this is really happening or only a dream. I will pinch myself and if it's only a dream I'll wake up and be safe.'

That was my escape route if I couldn't cope with the monsters and ghouls within the dream. I also began to find a way to disguise myself so that the monsters thought that I was one of them and not their victim. I can still remember the extraordinary solution I adopted of joining the Ghosts' Union and having a membership card that I showed to the nasties, who then left me alone or at least were friendly.

Now I think this may have been the most important event in my inner life. I had solved the most difficult problem that any imaginative man or woman ever faces: the enemy within had been recognised as part of myself that had split off and turned against me.

On the run again

Towards the end of the year the booming of guns grew louder, ration books were issued and, in September 1940, while Hitler was humming and ha-ing about his invasion plans for the British Isles, our little family evacuated briefly to my father's brother's house in Southwell near Nottingham.

It was a beautiful autumn and at the tender age of seven I formed lasting impressions of the horse chestnut trees, which I climbed in search of conkers, and the striking, rather awe-inspiring architecture of Southwell Minster. This early medieval building was full of spellbinding carvings of foliage from which strange faces stared out menacingly.

These were the happy memories. Unfortunately, there were far too many unhappy memories. My aunt obviously resented our staying with them and their young daughter, and my uncle was not going to intervene on our behalf. I was subjected to continual painful nagging and at the local school, because I was an intruder and foreigner, the children ganged up to bully me during playtime and after school. I had suffered from harassment and bullying at Petts Wood, but at least when I got home I could relax and forget about it. What made it worse this time was that my teacher made it quite clear she did not like me and I spent a lot of time standing among the coats outside the classroom, waiting to be chastised. However hard I tried to get a coloured picture on my schoolwork (there were several types from 'a good try' to 'excellent'), I always failed, even though on one occasion I wrote an enormously long essay.

In the end the headmaster decided to expel me for my restless behaviour. I found myself in tears in his office with my parents while my record of bad behaviour was discussed, but I was not expelled. My parents were furious at the treatment a seven-year-old child was getting from the staff and the children, just because he was different from the others.

Owing to the friction both at home and at school, my parents decided to move again to my mother's relatives in my beloved Framlingham.

2
An Anglican Anglo-Saxon in East Anglia

After my wretched experiences in Southwell, the arrival at the little market town of Framlingham, just before Christmas 1940, was one of those ecstatic states of delivery from evil that are found in the lives of the mystics and that form the basis of great fantasy literatures. It was a cloudy night and when the vehicle drew up at my uncle's house in the middle of a tight huddle of shops and houses I remember the moon was high in a sky suddenly clear of clouds.

We were welcomed into the White House, which was warm and 'countrified'. There was food and drink and lots of visitors, a new baby and two other young female cousins with two more male cousins near my own age just round the corner. My uncle was one of the last horse-collar makers in that part of England and outside there was a large barn full of straw and leather and tools; my grandmother's sweetshop stood next door. We were rather squeezed into the half of the house that housed my Uncle Jack and his family. The other half would soon be vacated so that we could live there.

A Christmas to remember

Much of the warmth and excitement was due to Christmas, which was fast approaching. On Christmas Eve I was so excited that I kept waking up to see if that magical being, Father Christmas, had called to leave presents for me. Then eventually I felt my stocking and the pillowcase at the end of the bed, and they were stuffed full of marvellous things. I can remember a harmonica and a box of stone shapes that could be arranged to make various patterns described in a booklet, but best of all I found I had a little magic lantern and three glass slides of Mickey Mouse adventures. My addiction to bright images on screens had begun with Saturday morning picture shows: serials, cartoons and animal stories.

The noise of the harmonica soon brought my father upstairs to warn me in solemn tones that Father Christmas had only just left my room and was still somewhere in the house. If I didn't instantly put the things away and go to sleep he might come back and take all my presents away. I was impressed with this reasoning and complied without objection. I still feel that good things that suddenly descend on me for no apparent reason are likely to disappear at any moment. Easy come, easy go.

I had almost caught Father Christmas in the act and so a precious illusion was preserved for at least another year. Jean, the girl next door in my early formative years in Petts Wood, had deeply shocked me earlier by telling me that fairies did not exist. That is another occasion where the emotional arousal was so great that the circumstances were permanently burned on my memory.

Beginning my childhood in the suburbs of what was then the largest city in the world, I was to finish it in a tiny country town cut off by the strictly controlled civilian life of the war. My father obtained a teaching job at the village of Haughley, twenty-three miles from Framlingham, and on weekends cycled over to be with my mother, sister and me. We soon moved

A studio portrait of Hilary and me.

18

into the other half of the White House and I was given the servant's room at the top of the kitchen stairs.

I often find myself back in this strange room during my dreams. The kitchen stairs were concealed behind a latched door and were very steep. The room itself was under the eaves with a sloping ceiling. One window looked out on the yard in front of the house over my uncle's workshop and small barn; the other, near my bed, showed the tops of the houses that backed on to ours.

The real thing . . . war

During the 'phoney war' of 1939–40 everyone was panicking and nothing much was happening. In 1941 came the real thing. Invasion was in the air, my father joined the Home Guard, blast walls were built in front of all exposed windows, rationing was strict and the roads were empty of most traffic. We had a Morrison shelter erected in the kitchen. This was a strong metal cage that provided protection against being crushed by falling masonry should the house be hit. The air raid siren sounded most nights but, apart from a cascade of incendiary bombs, which everyone rushed around putting out with their air-raid wardens' pumps and buckets, we were spared direct bombing. Nevertheless, night after night we would huddle downstairs in the metal cage as the German bombers droned overhead on their way across East Anglia to London or the Midlands.

The colourful, extravagant and independent world of the 1930s became grey, grim and communal, although this was not apparent to me as a child of eight. I was sent to the local C. of E. primary school, where I was chastised regularly for my ebullience and lack of seriousness. But since I loved reading and arguing with my parents, and had inherited considerable intelligence, I obtained a scholarship to Framlingham College. This establishment, a memorial to the brilliant Prince Albert, was a typical small Victorian English public school of the Thomas Arnold type.

An erratic education

My education had been far from smooth. Counting the schools where I had spent a few weeks during various evacuations, and those to which I had accompanied my mother or father for various reasons, I calculate that I had attended a dozen or so primary schools before I was accepted in the junior school of Framlingham College.

I had already attended numerous primary schools before I entered Framlingham College.

Life as one of the handful of local 'daybuts' at a residential school for the sons of the gentry and upper middle class was not easy but it was an improvement on the bullying of the peasant louts and offspring of the urban proletariat that I had endured for the previous two years.

My years of disrupted education had not meant that I was intellectually retarded. I was extremely good at mental arithmetic and at the age of six could do long division in my head. My correct answers were not marked as correct, however, because I didn't show 'the working'. Education is clearly designed to eliminate all intuitive, magical means of obtaining knowledge or achieving results.

At Framlingham College I was the brightest boy in my class for the first two years and still have the prizes I won for scholastic achievement. I was, like my sister, a voracious reader and from the age of seven saved up my pocket money to buy books. My mother was librarian at the local area school and I was able to supplement the local and college libraries with the books she brought home to classify. Apart from literary classics and science fiction, I had no use for fiction and I gave my parents the use of my fiction ticket until I left home for military service. Nature study and how things were made were my favourite interests and I roamed around in the countryside looking for nests, poking about in ponds and streams and bothering local inventors.

Lest it be thought that I was a withdrawn, anaemic, intellectual type, I should point out that I was also the champion tree climber in the area and had only one rival for running. I was a keen member of the dramatic society and the music teacher was so impressed by my musical gifts that he began to teach me to compose. Although I have always been repulsed by both masochism and sadism, and was unpopular for not joining any gangs, I loved rough and tumble and was an excellent wrestler.

A sign of my future calling

It was at this period that my talents as a public speaker first began to show themselves. I would get up on a bench in the cloakroom and make political speeches. These were first Tory, then Labour and, finally, raving Communist which, being young and socially oppressed (as all children are), was my favourite. Were these an early indication of my postmodern genius?

My extreme youth also meant that I had an unrealistic attitude to the opposite sex and can remember with embarrassment my naive romantic idealisation of a number of pretty girls who were not particularly responsive. Like most healthy and active young males, I had no interest in the facts of life at this time and studiously avoided those degenerate obsessive youths who were always sniggering in the toilets and who probably ended up giving compulsory sex-education classes for children.

A toffee-nosed Limey meets the Yanks

With the blackout and petrol rationing and all the young men away at the war, Framlingham was a rural paradise. Then, in 1942, the Yanks arrived, noisy, brash, insensitive, sex- and money-mad and looking for excitement. The effect on the locals was electrifying. Their wives and daughters were seduced with silk stockings and food parcels. Their quiet pubs were suddenly full of fighting foreigners who would later stagger home, emptying their stomachs and bowels in convenient doorways. The noise of their radios and convoys of trucks and Flying Fortresses overhead was amazing. Framlingham was situated within a few miles of several American airbases, as East Anglia was the ideal location for airfields.

I was only a young lad looking for fun myself and I thoroughly enjoyed the excitement that the visitors brought. I would cycle over to the nearby airfield at Parham and go on to the base without any sentries stopping me. I climbed all over the Fortresses, trying out the gun turrets and bringing home belts of live ammunition, which I tried unsuccessfully to convert into fireworks. The Yanks were so easy-going I used to queue up in the mess and get meals of strange foods, which are now, of course, our staple diet. I read copies of *Captain Marvel* comics in the crew's quarters and made many strong friendships among the Yanks, whose mental age was very close to my own. I was a very intelligent ten-year-old. I often look back on those unusual times with considerable nostalgia.

It was at this time that I first started smoking, introduced to this form of drug addiction by my Yankee 'buddies', who often gave me cartons of two hundred cigarettes. At the age of thirteen I gave up this filthy habit and swore that I would not smoke again until I was thirty. I kept my promise, and now smoke cigars with great enthusiasm.

I wonder where all those Yankee buddies of mine are now? Who knows? Maybe one or two have come through Christchurch as tourists and listened delightedly as I explain to them how America went wrong after their foolish rejection of monarchy and established religion. It's a pleasant thought.

Of course I don't hate Yanks: they're far too much like easily excited children. They do so many damn stupid things but they don't know any better. I still have hope that they will mature one day. The English suffer from the opposite problem – they're bright, lively and intelligent, but lacking in enthusiasm and willingness to give things a go.

Becoming one with nature

In Suffolk I was able to become well acquainted with wildlife. My father was a strong believer in the virtue of the Sunday Walk. Unlike my mother and me, he was not attracted to church rituals, preferring the wonders of nature to the mysteries of religion.

Saturday morning children's picture shows were a favourite treat and my admiration for the 'Red Indians' knew no bounds. Only Tarzan, an English aristocrat gone wild, rivalled the magnificent Redskins in my esteem. My wild man fantasy lasted well into my teens and I spent countless sunny days in the tops of tall trees dreaming that I lived in a different world.

The move into the country gave me the opportunity to explore every inch of the farmland and woodland around Framlingham. The ancient castle, with its crumbling walls, surrounding mounds and mere, was my favourite spot. I knew where all the birds were nesting, and what sort of creatures lived in the streams and ponds. I was sure that there was buried treasure somewhere near the castle walls and at least one story about the ghosts that haunted the castle got into the national press following my climbing through a high window and rummaging round in the old hall inside the walls.

During this period I wasn't an observer of nature: I felt as if I were *part* of it, an animal foraging around in his environment. The plants and trees were somehow magically connected with my existence. Later I came across the writer John Cowper Powys, whose rather bizarre novels exactly express my feeling for countryside.

This rural interlude soon came to an end. What began, in 1939–41, as a dramatic uprooting and nightmarish changes to everyday life, slowly became normality. The prewar days never returned, as the British fighting against the Nazis, for God, King and Empire, imperceptibly became the United Nations fighting for democracy. Democracy (or the people's will) replaced Christianity (or God's will) as our new unquestioned idol and the British Empire became an embarrassing memory to be replaced by the political myths of the two new superpowers, the United States and the Soviet Union, both of whom despised monarchy, established religion and imperialism.

As this photo shows, for Sunday walks we were scrubbed and polished, and put into our best clothes, before solemnly making our way along country lanes and footpaths.

3

The class struggle

When the war ended, our little family left Framlingham and returned to our semi-detached in Petts Wood. At first we had to stay with friends in makeshift accommodation because the woman and her grown-up daughter who had been given the use of our house under a compulsory requisitioning scheme refused to budge, even though our needs were much more pressing. When we finally got back home and my father had repaired all the damage done by the squatters, we could look forward to a more settled existence.

Destined for lower-middle-class values

Framlingham College had given my father a reference to use in obtaining a place for me in one of the élite public schools in South London. But although he was a teacher, and came from a middle-class background, my father was a radical socialist and did not think that I should necessarily be given any extra advantages over other children. Instead of using this reference, which was apparently rather glowing, and would probably have secured me a place at Dulwich College, he sent me to the local state grammar school.

Bromley Grammar School for Boys was essentially a school for those who had passed the IQ test and wanted to better themselves through intellectual achievement. Little or no effort was wasted in teaching us discipline or character development and the cultural side was almost entirely absent. Over and over again we were praised for our intelligence and encouraged to work hard to pass exams so that we could rise above our parents in terms of salaried employment.

This was a shock to me, coming from a college of young gentlemen where manners and character and knowing how to lead others were more important than swotting or salary or pushing to get some 'room at the top'. Back in the aggressive, pushy world of London, dumped into an uncongenial school, I found my career taking a decided turn for the worse. In the past one's fate was decided by which family one was born into, but today one's fate is decided by which school tie one is wearing. I had missed out on both counts, although I almost made it on the 'old boy network'. I think it's obvious from my manners and attitudes that I am almost a gentleman but not quite. This rather difficult situation produced a lot of tension that I did not resolve until much later.

The end of the war was accompanied by the dramatic change in the political structure of Britain that accompanied the Labour Party victory in the 1945 elections. I had been in a socially difficult situation during the election campaign that last year at Framlingham College, since I appeared to be the only boy in the entire school who wanted a Labour victory. In a country school for young gentlemen, where the only heretics were Liberal Party supporters, a socialist was a kind of monster from the urban cesspits.

At Bromley Grammar School for Boys.

For both hereditary and environmental reasons I am destined to be a radical; I can see no alternative. My father was an unusual man driven by a strong sense of social justice, which caused him to break from his petty bourgeois family and go to London to teach children in the slums. He was sensitive, rather unsociable and lacking confidence in relationships with the opposite sex. There was a closer bond between him and my sister, who has a similar temperament. I am rather more like my mother.

With a mother who was called 'Golly' or 'Fire-Engine Fanny' in her youth and a father who raised pigs to put himself through teachers' college and who was a member of the radical Yellow Book Club during the controversial 1930s, my inheritance was not that of a trendy who copied his fellows. My upbringing so far had included sudden shifts from town to country and back again, and from peace to war and back again, compounded by attendance at a host of schools. It was not likely that I would easily conform.

Life at Bromley Grammar School was not satisfying my need for

Framlingham College.

STUDIO SAPIENTIA CRESCIT

Name... *L. B. Channell* ... Form *II A*

Age *11.1* ... Average Age of Form *11.11*

Number of Boys in Form... *22*

	Term	Exam	Final Order
Place in Form	*6*	*13*	*9*

Rather a nuisance: if he were more sensible I feel he could become quite a useful member of society.

.... *L. W. H. Hull* .... House Master

I quite agree with his House master's comment. Is capable of very good work + does not make the most of his ability.

.... *R. W. Kirkman* .... Head Master

The Next Term will begin on *17ᵗʰ January, 1944*

9.A. M 18 January 1944 — day boys

As this 1943 report shows, I did not fit into the established education system.

meaning. Attempts to motivate me to feats of scholastic brilliance by appeals to greed and security (in the form of a well-paid job) fell on stony ground and every report said 'could do better' in various ways. I didn't know what I wanted to be, but neither nurture nor nature had predisposed me towards seeking security at any price. During my six years of secondary education, I led the real class war in the classroom. I was not an unhappy, disturbed child; I was a bloody nuisance.

Salvation through the Boy Scouts

Then I stumbled on my vocation and my life was transformed. I can't even remember what caused me to attend that first meeting: all I know is that joining the Second Petts Wood Scout Troop altered my life permanently.

Many accounts have been written of the experience of salvation from sin and the sense of relief that comes from being born again. Enlightenment can take many forms. Feminists of both sexes suddenly realise that they are liberated from the traditional sexual stereotypes and pursue homosexual stereotypes instead. Such conversions are followed by a great release of enthusiasm and dedication to the cause. It is obvious that I have not been

The Second Petts Wood Scout Group, in 1949. I am second from left.

released from original sin and nor have I thrown off the oppressive burden of heterosexuality. My release was from 'civilisation and its discontents'.

As a latent existentialist I had come across an association that had no purpose whatsoever. In no way could learning how to splice ropes or cook over a camp fire in pouring rain, or how to recognise animal tracks, or build bridges with wood and string or sleep under canvas during frosty nights be seen as political, economic, religious or even faintly rational behaviour. It was not even being done in the conscious anticipation that civilisation would shortly collapse. Looking back now, I can see that not only are the activities of the Scout movement very similar to those of primitive, nomadic hunter-gatherers, but even their social structures and belief systems are surprisingly similar.

I had left the maternal nest and was becoming a man for the first time. Initiation rites, tough, uncomfortable conditions, adventurous hikes using ordnance survey maps and keeping a log, but, best of all, the campfires at night with the chants and horror stories. I found I had a gift for storytelling and even as a tenderfoot could keep the attention of the troop for hours and was at my best when leading the ecstatic chants round the fire. The primitive shaman or medicine man that lay deeply buried in me under hundreds of years of civilisation was conjured into life. For a few brief, wonderful years, although forced to endure an education for a future in which I did not believe, at least I came alive at weekends and during the holidays.

A sensitive new-age guy?

Lest it be thought that my interest in strenuous sport in the form of athletics and swimming and love of the Great Outdoors had made me into a 'hollow man' with no subtle feminine interior life, I must assure my readers that this was not the case. When puberty struck, with its usual violence, I must admit I was thrown off balance. I was suddenly interested in the artistically posed nudes in *Lilliput*, the excellent little 'gentleman's magazine' of the 1940s. I was also being deepened by a craving for music and poetry.

The potential was there. At the insistence of my mother, I had been learning to play the piano since I was eleven. I was not enthusiastic about practising but looked forward to my weekly lessons, perhaps because I was allowed to spend an hour or two afterwards listening wide-eyed as my teacher's husband, who was an inventor, explained his latest gadget. But the piano was just about my least preferred instrument; I would much rather have learnt to play the trombone. Unfortunately this was not my mother's most preferred instrument. I got as far as coming second in a local music festival in Orpington with my impassioned rendition of a Chopin mazurka. I gradually lost interest after this. Now if I had come first . . .

In my early teens only two types of music interested me – light classical and hot jazz. I had no liking for swing and the crass popular music of the time. The 'wireless' was my source of musical education as my parents had few records in the house and were not concertgoers. I discovered that most of the light classical music I found myself whistling on my early morning paper round was composed by one man, Gioacchino Rossini, who became my musical idol for a few years.

Escape from suburbia into fantasy

Like poor Don Quixote, my taste for fantasy was also growing. I devoured the short stories of H.G. Wells and progressed to his novels and any other science fiction I could find in the local library. In those days librarians re-garded SF with horror but had to allow 'classics' like Wells and Verne shelf space. My taste in fantasy matured into an obsession with Milton's *Paradise Lost*, Dante's *Inferno* and Spenser's *Faerie Queene*, strange choices for an adolescent youth. I was so enthralled that I was slipshod with the wretched, juvenile homework my schoolteachers kept setting me. They did not appre-ciate the fact that I was 'educating' myself my own way.

I founded the school Music Society, revived the moribund Debating Society, was an active member of the Drama Society and Air Training Corps and was a good athlete. Moreover, in the all-important General School Cer-tificate I got one of the best results in the school.

'Education is wasted on this boy'

This phrase appeared regularly in my teachers' reports at this time. I ended up near the bottom of the class in most subjects, including English. I was one of the only boys in the history of the school who was never made a prefect in spite of being three years in the sixth form and doing well in exams and in athletics.

I have never managed to work out why I have had such a difficult life. I have had little if any co-operation from my superiors and almost no one has ever thought it worthwhile to encourage me or to sponsor my talents. The nearest I can get to an explanation is that they 'don't like my attitude'. Perhaps it is my irritating combination of contrariness, cheerfulness, scep-tical otherworldliness and inability to appear sincere.

The headmaster of Bromley Grammar School for Boys was just like

Captain Queeg in *The Caine Mutiny*, a film I only saw some time after I left school. It was a real case of *déjà vu*. When his paranoiac outbursts occurred he would stalk round the school building jingling his keys. The teachers themselves showed such fear that we all kept very quiet as the poor deranged figure strode past the classrooms. Unfortunately whenever the inspectors called he was the personification of charm and good humour.

He and I came into headlong collision towards the end of my time at the school. He blamed the sixth form for leaving a mess after an old boys' function and would not believe our denials of responsibility. He made the shocking decision to cancel the school sports so we decided that we might as well commit the crime for which we were being so severely punished. I organised a party to hide in the school until it was closed and then to put red flags on all the pinnacles. There was an eruption of volcanic proportions, with pictures in the local newspaper, and this time everything was cancelled. The head insisted that whoever did it should own up. To his credit, the head boy joined me in the principal's office.

During my last year the head had withheld my application for a university scholarship paper without even informing me, on the grounds that he considered it a waste of time my even taking the exam. Since my marks the previous year in the Higher School Certificate had been pretty good, this was a dirty trick. The odd thing was that he and I were the only two people from the school who regularly frequented the second-hand bookshop in Bromley.

Discovering Berlioz

It was in this wonderful scruffy treasure house that I came across an old 78 rpm record of Sir Hamilton Harty conducting the *Carnival Romain* overture of Hector Berlioz. At first the music was so unexpected in its abrupt changes of tempo and rhythm and drawn-out themes that I had to listen to it many times before it clicked. Once that happened I became a Berlioz devotee. It was not just his wonderful skill with the orchestra, but also his passionate personal and ironic style of writing that completely enthralled me.

During my last year at school I discovered Mahler's symphonies and Schubert's string quartets. Mahler's second symphony, the *Resurrection*, was the only one available on record and took up about ten discs. I had borrowed a Lewisham public library ticket from a girlfriend and would cycle the ten miles or so to Lewisham and back with the heavy and fragile burden on my carrier. Since it was often raining and there were still tramlines in those far-off days, this was a perilous proceeding.

I stayed behind after school to use the gramophone in the school hall. The glorious sound of the *Resurrection* Symphony filled the hall and I trembled with excitement. Since then I seem to have always had a daemon urging me to resurrect myself and ascend or levitate by defying gravity in all its forms. This was a most uplifting occasion.

A teenage misogynist

I was properly scared of becoming entangled with young women. I saw too many of my friends 'get hooked' and lose their innocent self-centredness by becoming prematurely 'adult'. I had no desire to 'grow up' that way. I watched with horror as my sister perfected the art of leading earnest young men on to the point of infatuation and even proposals of marriage and then rejecting them.

It was horribly like the *Just William* books by local author Richmal Compton, which I devoured as a young boy and which described pretty well the general heartlessness of teenage girls towards teenage boys.

Although I was only too easily aroused by the sight of attractive female faces and figures, I repressed my libido or sublimated it into reading and listening to classical music. I was grateful that my school was not co-educational. I had a sister and a mother at close quarters at home: I didn't need more women around during the day as well. As the only boy at my school who was an outspoken misogynist I became fairly notorious among the local girls' schools. During my last year I began to modify my intransigent attitude and dated a few local girls.

Torn between love and freedom

I was torn between the desire to control my own destiny and the desire to lose myself in erotic union, the age-old struggle between love and freedom, and I haven't changed much over the years.

Around the age of seventeen I began a series of cautious approaches to girls who were showing obvious interest in my well-developed physique (I came second in the Tarzan competition at a Butlins Holiday Camp in 1952) and devil-may-care attitude to life. Until I met the young lady from Lewisham, the girls I had been out with, including two Audreys, had been calculating flirts with fluff between their ears, and going out once or twice was enough for both of us.

The girl whose library ticket I had borrowed was the only one whose sensuality matched mine, but alas she and I had little else in common. We

This photo was taken in August 1949, not long before my 17th birthday.

felt the flames of lust consuming us and we were both rather scared of the consequences. She felt it important to end our relationship. She came from the same school as my sister and I suspected interference from my sometimes rather manipulative sibling. I wouldn't have agreed so easily if we had had more psychological affinity.

I did, however, have one good female friend who had left school early, earned her own living and lived alone with her mother. Betty ran a kind of salon for young men who would gather around and impress her with accounts of their heroic exploits. She was such a cool customer I used to call her 'Iceberg', a name she still employs in her correspondence to me almost a half century later.

I needed a girlfriend with both a sympathetic psyche and a responsive soma. I loved to talk about music and art and politics and religion and was looking for companionship as well as passion. At the end-of-year annual dance with our sister school I met Monica, whom I had seen a few days before in their school play. She had been dressed as a medieval minstrel and the combination of her dramatic Pre-Raphaelite features and dark contralto voice had impressed me.

At the dance we talked about music and I saw her home afterwards. She was an extremely reserved girl and I was not sure if she was interested in me or not. This was the end of my school 'sentence' and I was about to set off on another backpacking trip to the Riviera so I doubted if we would meet again.

Such unstructured travel or wanderlust, which had been nurtured during my Scouting days, led to my being the only boy in the school who adventured abroad with a backpack during the hols. Sleeping in a tent, living on bread and jam and often spending a full day waiting for a lift from mainly Anglophobic Frenchmen was well worth the reward of a few weeks on the Mediterranean coast with my friend Louis. This was a world miles apart from the dull weather and pettiness, and lower-middle-class snobbery of Bromley Grammar School.

4

The navigator

When I finally returned home, sun-tanned and pimply, I found my call-up papers for National Service had arrived and I had missed the induction date. My parents had informed them I was overseas but nothing had been heard back from the War Office. After waiting a few weeks I finally contacted them and was interviewed for the Royal Air Force. To my amazement they considered me officer material and sent me off to basic training and then to pilots' training school.

In my officer's uniform with the family, 1951.

Monica was keen to see me during the few days before I was willingly ripped from my mother's bosom to do my bit for King and Country. So began an important relationship that lasted seventeen years but did not survive my rather sudden transition from trendy, anarchistic academic, to bohemian, monarchistic wizard.

My experiences during my time in compulsory military service were not as much fun as backpacking or Scouting, but they were a damn sight more enjoyable than my experiences during compulsory secular education. At least I was not being manipulated into believing a load of rubbish about the importance of getting a well-paid job. Honour and loyalty were more valued and I didn't have to believe in anything. I just had to do what I was told and tell others what to do. That was easy.

'Ours not to reason why' is a philosophy I can perfectly well understand. I also enjoy 'reasoning why', at the right time and place, and loved the debates I organised at school. But I held (and still hold) very unfashionable opinions about 'why'. There's often an embarrassed silence, then everyone carries on as if I'd said nothing.

From English officer to Canadian cadet

After flying and gliding in the ATC I really enjoyed being taught to fly in the wonderful old Tiger Moths. Unfortunately in the middle of the pilot training programme all of us whose surnames began with A to D were suddenly informed that we were to be navigators and would be sent to Canada for training as part of NATO. The alternative was to lose our officer status and aircrew training and be reclassified as the lowest rank. I, too, was surprised since I had no liking for maths and had actually failed the selection test for navigators. But this was the life of action, not analysis.

We spent almost a year in Winnipeg, one of the coldest cities on earth. The base was some miles out of town and the camp cinema had just been closed for refurbishment. We were reduced in the ranks to officer cadets, as that was the way the Royal Canadian Air Force trained their aircrew, but at least our pay was not reduced, though we were herded into overheated barracks and a cavernous mess and lost our batmen.

I found solace in the record shops in Winnipeg. The new LPs were within my financial grasp and were spectacularly better than the old 78 rpm records, especially for Mahler.

To my surprise, I thoroughly enjoyed training to be a navigator. There were three slight snags. First, there was no radar in Canada at that time; second, we were quite close to the northern magnetic pole; and third, most

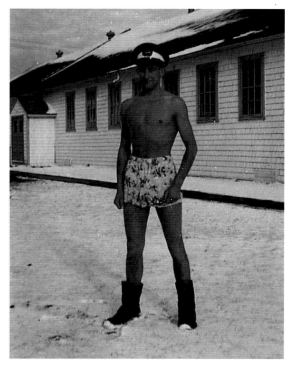

A pilot officer stranded in Winnipeg.

In full flying gear, 1951.

of the terrain we flew over was tundra and the lakes changed shape according to the season.

We were taught a kind of primitive night navigation using bubble sextants in a bouncing aircraft to get a fix on three stars (if we could see the sky, of course). The calculations were rather complicated and had to be done as fast as possible but, by the time we found out where we were, we were miles away. Owing to the uncertain nature of the terrain, it wasn't much use trying to find out where we were during the day by looking at the ground and map reading. We were sometimes reduced to flying low over the Canadian Pacific Railway line to read the names of remote stations. Near the magnetic pole we were forced to use a gyroscopic compass that had to be painstakingly reset every half hour or so.

No wonder some of my colleagues landed in the United States by mistake. If all else failed we would tune in on a radio programme and fly along the beam. The only snag here was that one or two aircraft crashed into the broadcasting mast. Also, severe icing-up on the wings badly affected the aerodynamics and was a source of considerable concern to me.

Hitch-hiking by air

Before we graduated and went back to Britain to be trained all over again using radar, we had a two-week furlough. I had found that if I turned up in uniform at an American air base there was a good chance I could get a lift somewhere in a transport plane. This was the life! I was aiming at a tour of the United States. Unfortunately the only lift I could get from Winnipeg was in completely the wrong direction, north to Edmonton.

I enjoyed the sight of the aurora borealis but I was relieved to find a plane going south. What a lift — it took me to Florida! From Pensacola, in the Gulf of Mexico, I hitched by road to Northern Florida and down the coast to the Keys and back to Miami, where I got another preposterously long lift, this time to Los Angeles with a night's stopover in Houston. I was in LA just long enough to hitch down to Mexico and back, and to experience the biggest earthquake in LA for many years before I travelled up the coast road to San Francisco.

This was a city I really liked. Most American towns lacked what is now called ambience. I was spellbound by San Francisco, but when I tried to get back to my faraway outpost in Canada by waiting for a lift at Edwards air base there was nothing doing. Time was running out and I had thousands of miles to cover. I was lucky and eventually got back, via Salt Lake City, just in time. My journey had been an epic odyssey of which I was quietly proud. No one else had been further than just over the border.

Back in England we were told that our Canadian observers' wings were useless and we were trained all over again with radar and slightly faster aircraft, Wellingtons and Doves. Then we were also informed that, apart from a few aircraft in Coastal Command, pilots were now using automatic navigation aids and we were redundant. I didn't mind: I went home to wait for my posting.

My sudden rise in authority

By some administrative blunder I was posted as flying wing adjutant to a fighter station at Duxford near Cambridge with two squadrons of Meteors. This was fairly senior desk job for an experienced pilot. The wing-commander in charge of flying, an ex-Battle of Britain hero, was mightily put out by the arrival of a 'sprog' National Service navigator as his right-hand man. I did my best, holding parades and helping to organise the surprising visit of Marshal Tito. Living in the officers' mess, I had two batwomen to bring me a cuppa in the morning, make the bed and clean my shoes – luxury!

But, after a few months, the wing commander finally got a proper replacement and I was no longer needed. The group captain in charge of RAF Duxford asked me into his office and said he could arrange my early release. (*No one* gets early release from National Service.) But I had to decline his kind offer as I had already earmarked my remaining two months' pay: I was saving up for a trip to the place of my dreams, Greece.

My pilgrimage

My trip to Italy and Greece in the autumn of 1953 was a wonderful experience. I took the train through Italy to Brindisi and then boat across the Adriatic and through the Corinth Canal to Piraeus and Athens. I had my beloved *Blue Guide*, and settled into the tiny but convivial youth hostel in Athens.

The civil war had only recently ended and inflation was so bad that everyone dealing with money had to carry small sacks. Summer was over, rain made the old stones shine and there were very few tourists. I felt like a devout Christian visiting the Holy Land. This was my sacred place and I trod the stones of Mycenae, Olympus, Epidaurus, Knossos and the Parthenon with awe and reverence. This was where my world began.

My travels seemed to have considerable impact on Monica, who shared my desire to take off and roam. We became closely attached and began a series of short sorties out of England into Europe. Monica was training to be a teacher, specialising in music for young children, and I got my first job.

5
I become a wage-slave and get married

I would have been quite happy to have stayed at home for a while to rest up and continue my programme of self-education, but my parents were adamant. No way was I going to avoid work by living on the dole!

'Dickensian' was probably the best term to describe the small firm of Herring, Dewick and Cripps, paper merchants of Coleman Street in the City of London, where I began my first proper job. Since I was one of their reps and visited various printers to persuade them to buy our paper, I was only in the office for the first hour of the day and the last. We sat perched on high stools in the outer office while 'Mr Arthur', legendary last member of the founding dynasty, entertained in his private office in the rear.

As paper prices were fixed, this was little more than a PR job and I had so much spare time that I was able to explore London, catch up on my private education and make regular visits to Tower Hill at lunchtimes to listen to the orators. Donald Soper, the Methodist preacher who influenced such excellent New Zealand speakers as David Lange and Bob Lowe, was at this time still bellowing across the cobbles and dealing with secular humanists, fascists and Marxists with equal skill. My own favourite, who became a personal friend, was Bannister, a slight, rather scruffy figure with a nicotine-stained moustache. His speciality was the ironic demolition of all points of view, though his passionate love of Shakespeare and love of being true to his roots made him a monarchist and British imperialist, *faute de mieux*. I think it is rather obvious that I owe much of my style as a public speaker to his benign influence.

Monica was at the famous Goldsmith's College, combining teacher training with music, and she joined the Royal Choral Society. At every opportunity we would take off for the weekends and holidays, usually staying at youth hostels or camping out. During the summer holidays we went overseas. Our trips to the west coast of Ireland by bicycle, the Netherlands by motor scooter and Spain by train (a rare destination in the mid-1950s) were wonderful.

Married without children

We planned to give up our jobs and take off round the world. Being unmarried could lead to difficulties in foreign lands, so in 1956 we decided to get

married. We had no plans for a home or children; this was a travelling partnership. Our honeymoon was spent on our motor scooter in Yugoslavia, as that was the year Tito opened up the country to tourists.

Monica and me on our wedding day, 1956, and, farewelled by Monica's sister Gwenda, off on our scooter honeymoon.

Meanwhile we moved into a flat in Notting Hill and enjoyed the rich cultural life of London in the mid-1950s. It was a wonderful time for music. At last Mahler's genius was being recognised and we attended many first English performances of his symphonies. Britten and Tippett were at the height of their powers and we were able to be at the first full performance of Berlioz's greatest opera, *The Trojans*. I had been a member of the world's only Berlioz Society for some years; a dozen of us were really keen fans.

Our other chief joy was the National Film Theatre on the South Bank. Previously we had been to 'art films' by Ingmar Bergman and others, but it wasn't until we went to see Eisenstein's *Ivan the Terrible* that we were converted on the spot to the realisation that the cinema was the greatest art form of this century. We haunted the NFT for the following years and particularly appreciated the black-and-white silent films of the 1920s. With a few rare exceptions, I still prefer these to colour and sound films.

This was also the time of the Campaign for Nuclear Disarmament. I attended the first meetings and we went on the first march to Aldermaston. I was attracted by the non-political, ecumenical, religious leadership and the lack of angry resentment in the demonstrations and marches. Later the anti-religious Bertrand Russell managed to gain control and the movement became a disaster.

Around the world in eighty years

We had been saving hard for our trip and held a 'soirée and jumble sale' for all our effects. Our friends, mainly Australian, bought most of our stuff and, early in 1958, we set sail in time for the opening of the great Brussels Expo, which, in hindsight, seems to have been part of the early stages of the European Common Market. The new city of Rotterdam, replacing the one flattened by Nazi bombs out of sheer spite, was all glass, aluminium and fluorescent lighting. It was a vision of the multinational, multicultural, characterless future that we both dreaded. Carrying everything we needed in our backpacks, we hitched across Europe into Italy and into the sunshine.

At last we had plenty of time to wander freely without having to hurry back to work. (In those days our friends regarded our kind of travelling as quite mad. Of course our Australian and New Zealand friends were doing the same thing, as O.E. – overseas experience – was becoming perfectly acceptable in the Antipodes.) The luxury of two months in Italy gave us time to visit many of the fascinating galleries, churches and Roman and Greek ruins. Sicily was spectacular, especially the Greek temples and Byzantine mosaics.

Once again I was crossing the Adriatic to Greece, this time with my new travelling companion, who never complained and who loved roughing it as much as I did. We spent two months in Greece and the Aegean Islands, visiting such magical places as Delphi, Olympia and Knossos. We rented a lovely little house in Mykonos for a pittance and lived on the delicious local food. Much better than meat and two vegies, although I missed English puddings. No other cuisine in the world comes close to the variety and taste of English sweets.

Monica and I depart for our O.E.

We crossed the border into Turkey at a time of financial crisis: our money was worth almost ten times more than the usual exchange rate. We could have stayed at the Istanbul Hilton for the cost of a bed and breakfast in

Among the ruins at Persepolis.

England. I swam the Bosphorus. This was the life! Turkey was beautiful and interesting beyond our wildest expectations.

In Iran we found temporary accommodation in the changing rooms of the city's swimming pool, putting our sleeping bags and small airbeds on the concrete floor. The British Council was happy to have us teach evening classes in English literature and Monica was engaged as an infant teacher at the British Embassy school where the Shah sent his children. We soon rented a modern flat and settled down to spend some time resting up and earning money for the next leg of our world tour.

Back to dear old Blighty, and beyond

At the end of the academic year I went to Paris to buy a new car, a very cheap new car, a Citroen 2CV. Since it was duty-free it only cost £200. I had never driven a car before, only my motor scooter. In Tehran I had shown officials my motorcycle licence and they issued me with an international driving licence – lucky me! I can't describe the horror of my first experience of driving a car, especially across Paris – and particularly negotiating the roundabout at the Arc de Triomphe – but I got the car to England without accident and we spent a lovely summer there.

We set off for Iran with the numerous visas and car documentation that would enable us to drive down to the Mediterranean and through Spain to Morocco, Algeria, Tunisia, Egypt, Jordan and Iraq (a trip of a lifetime). At the Algerian border, however, we were told we needed a 'carnet de passage'. Since Algeria was then part of France we had been informed by the people at Citroen that no special carnet was needed. We frantically wired Paris. No reply. We waited a week in the dreary desert and headed back around the Mediterranean again. Bloody French!

Having retraced the road back to Northern Italy, we were on the usual route back to Iran, even though thousands of miles of the road through Yugoslavia and Turkey and Iran were unsealed, corrugated and extremely dusty. Owning our own car enabled us to make weekend and holiday trips around the deserts of Iran.

A Christian teaching Jews in an Islamic country

I got an extra job, teaching various subjects in English at a secondary school for Jews who had escaped the Ba'athite persecutions in Iraq. A Christian teaching Jews in a school in a Muslim country! The holiday situation was extremely complicated. All schools closed on Friday, the holy day for Islam

Istanbul, September 1959.

*Mount Ararat provides the background in this photo of Monica
and the 2CV taken on the Turkish-Iranian border.*

and the Jews had Saturday as their holy day but I couldn't persuade them to
let me keep the Christian Sabbath as well.

Monica gets sick

Halfway through the year Monica developed a persistent cough that was
incorrectly diagnosed by the English doctor. An Iranian doctor finally found
she had a nasty case of tuberculosis. Since the climate in Tehran was excellent, high and dry, and we liked and trusted our new doctor, I administered

the injections and cooked the meals while she rested all day. She recovered amazingly quickly, as the X-rays showed.

We travelled back home again by air, with the aim of buying a second-hand American car and driving it back to Tehran for resale in a country where petrol was extremely cheap. In England Monica went for a medical check-up. To our surprise, the doctors said the X-rays didn't look good. She must go back into hospital to convalesce.

What a catastrophe! How could we go back to Iran if she was really sick? We decided to wait a month and look at the X-rays again. Annoyingly, the doctors steadfastly refused to take another X-ray for three months, so we were more or less obliged to stay in England. While Monica was convalescing, I decided I would go to university to 'get a bit of paper'.

First, though, I had return overland to Iran to settle our affairs. The previous year my sister's husband had died suddenly and she needed a break, so we went on a short holiday to France. On the way through Belgium, where petrol prices were astronomical, I bought a four-year-old gas-guzzling Chevrolet for a song. I drove this back to Tehran, but the long trip across Europe, followed by thousands of kilometres of unsealed, corrugated roads from Ankara, was tough on the car. My spare set of tyres were starting to run out as I neared the Iranian border. Luckily I found a Turk who swapped a couple of retreads for my authentic Chevvy bonnet mascot.

Back in Tehran I collected some money owing to me from my teaching, sold the car at a good profit, disposed of the furniture and said goodbye to all our friends. Loading up the Citroen with our favourite treasures, I began the trip back to England. I wish I could forget the nightmarish return journey, especially the bit where my lights failed crossing a remote pass in the Alps and I drove through using the lights of a friendly lorry driver.

A place at university

I had matriculated with credits in seven subjects and had 'A' levels in history, English and French. This was more than enough to get in to a university, but maths was required for any science course, and Latin was required for any arts course. I had disliked both subjects intensely and had missed the necessary credit in GCE maths by a single mark.

No one wanted me and it was getting very late in the year so I was overjoyed when I picked up my mail at the poste restante as I passed through Istanbul and found I had been accepted at Leeds University for an experimental honours course combining psychological and social theory, limited to a dozen undergraduates.

I had just started at Leeds when the doctors finally took an X-ray of Monica's lungs and found there was nothing there! I suspect xenophobia had preventing them from a realistic appraisal of the first X-ray and made them advise us not to return to Iran. We were both furious. But we had burnt our boats.

The years in Leeds were highly stimulating. We managed to find an attic flat and, with Monica teaching and my study grant, we could even afford car/camping trips in the Citroen during the holidays. What a difference from the mediocrity of secondary school. We were trusted to study at our own pace. No more odious homework or compulsory books, and we were actually encouraged to question our teachers during tutorials. This was learning the way I liked it.

I threw myself into student existence with a vengeance and revitalised the rather ordinary Film Society by fancy promotion techniques, and by combining screenings with other clubs and societies. I introduced silent and experimental films and started film festivals. Film Soc. became the largest and richest club on the campus. I also edited a film magazine that not only contained articles written by students but also reviewed all the films opening in Leeds that week. Politically I was now an anarchist but not a socialist disguised as one. In my opinion, only tramps, itinerant tradesmen, street performers and backpackers with no property or regular employment, are true anarchists.

I stage a cultural coup

In my final year I organised a 'coup' by the leaders of the various cultural groups to improve the funding of their activities by the student union. The sporting and social activities had been lavishly supported but there was almost no funding for culture. A large number of us stood for election to the union and most got in. The new body voted for the establishment of a cultural affairs officer and my name was proposed. There was no such executive officer in any other university in Britain and the president was keen for me to accept. Although I was in my final year, I decided to take on the job and I restructured the union's funding system so that the clubs and societies flourished and dozens of magazines appeared. I was briefly a TV star when we took part in the first *University Challenge* series and our team won.

I was worried about what sort of degree I would get. My course was an experimental one and the Department of Sociology had never awarded a first-class pass. I really studied hard and through my self-education programme had a fairly broad background of general knowledge.

My father dies suddenly – more medical incompetence

I was all 'psyched up' and had taken the first couple of papers when news came from home that my father had had a serious heart attack. As I only had a couple more weeks to go I stayed in Leeds and planned to go home as soon as the exams were over. The next day I got a phone call to say that he had died. The funeral was being held during the weekend so that I could be there.

This was a great shock and completely threw me, as he had no history of any serious bad health. His first symptoms had been misdiagnosed by his doctor and he was allowed to go up and down stairs. This was what finished him. I was getting more and more angry with doctors who seemed unable to make quite simple diagnoses. I stay well away from most of them and the ones I do get on with share my distrust of the medical profession.

Imagine the difficulty of rushing down to London and back in the middle of taking my finals and seeing my mother distraught with grief; she never recovered from the shock. My head was so full of material in preparation for the exams that I couldn't really absorb my father's death. When it did finally sink in I felt only loss, no guilt, since he and I had got on well. He never tried to live through me and I never did things just to please him. I wished he had lived to see me pass my finals. He always considered me too impulsive (like my mother) and my success would have shown him that I could knuckle under and get down to it if I was involved enough. I like to remember my father surrounded by the London slum children whom he organised to make gardens on old bombsites.

Discrimination – sexism and ageism

In spite of all this, I got an upper second honours degree. I was disappointed but was really put out when I heard, in the following year, that a female student was given a first. I had never seen any signs in her of originality of thought or clarity of expression. Knowing the ideological bias of sociologists, I suspected sexual discrimination.

When I tried to apply for a postgraduate research grant I hit another form of discrimination – ageism. There were simply no grants available to any students over the age of thirty. I was finally offered a small research grant to study cinema at Cine Citta in Rome. I don't know if we could have lived on it, and I had heard rumours that the Italian government was unreliable in paying grants.

A change of fortune

Then came another of those sudden reversals of fortune that have marked my life so far. I saw an ad for the position of a tutor/organiser community arts for the Adult Education Board of the University of Western Australia. Thinking that my unique experience at Leeds University might qualify me, I replied and was interviewed. I got the job even though it was a tenured lectureship and I had graduated only weeks before. This was exceptional, even for me.

I told my mother of the offer and of my reluctance to take up the post if she needed me to be close. She urged me to take it since it was an excellent opportunity. I was so impressed with her sacrifice that I vowed to repay the debt some day.

Culture commissar

Life as an academic in Perth could not have been more different than life as a student in Leeds – from an attic flat in the cold and grimy north of England to a house on the beach beside the Indian Ocean where the sun was always shining and the winters were warmer than most English summers. I had a brand-new Holden as part of the job, which involved travelling with cultural groups all over the huge state of Western Australia, which dwarfs even Texas.

I found something of a panic on my arrival in October 1963. John Birman, deputy director of the Adult Education Board and the executive officer of the annual Festival of Perth, was about to go overseas on his sabbatical and I was expected to take over the whole complex festival in two weeks' time! I was not only a complete novice in running events of

Life beside the Indian Ocean – posing on the beach in Perth.

this size, but I knew nothing about Australia, let alone the way local artistic circles operated. I struggled through, learning what to do from the secretary (who was not keen to see anyone doing her beloved boss's job) and from the departmental accountant, a 'dinkum Aussie' who took nothing seriously and knew everything about everyone. All went well.

After the festival, which was held over two months at the hottest time of the year, I took a short break and then began to tackle the community arts programme. Organising tours of Western Australia by musicians and actors was a regular part of my job.

Bringing cinema classics to WA

As there were no film societies in Perth, I started one in the city and set up others in the country towns, bringing the films over from the eastern states. I gave adult education lectures in sociological theory, which may have been the first in Australasia, and also in film appreciation; these were a definite first. I also pioneered the idea of a film school with the help of the Australian Government Film Unit.

I was responsible for planning the next Festival of Perth and this gave me the chance to upgrade the presentation and design. The 1965 festival was a great success. John Birman was now back from his sabbatical and I was to be his assistant during the next festival and would be responsible for the films. Monica had found a good teaching job and we had bought an old house in Mosman Park, now a very expensive part of town.

A very unbusinesslike enterprise

In late 1965 I had the idea of a joint venture with the owner of a nice little cinema in Dalkeith, an attractive suburb near the centre of town. The cinema was running down owing to lack of patronage and I proposed running a set-up something like the National Film Theatre in London, which would be called the International Film Theatre. I would provide the films and programme notes and the owner would act as manager/projectionist. No cinema in Perth was then showing quality films on a regular basis.

To my surprise, neither the director nor the deputy director of the Adult Education Board was in favour of the idea. It seemed they didn't regard films as a worthy art form, and films were included in the festival mainly on the basis of ease of presentation and income earning. They would not agree to any community arts programme involvement. Nor was I allowed to be a commercial partner should I go ahead on my own. This was particularly

WEST AUSTRALIAN NEWSPAPERS

Monica and I and a bunny girl are surprised by the camera at the Dolphin Theatre in Perth, November 1966.

unfair as many well-paid senior academics did consultant work for very high fees and with no risk. I would have to take personal responsibility for all losses but couldn't claim for any profits, which would go to the cinema owner.

I went ahead in 1966 in spite of these ridiculous terms, and IFT was a huge success. The cinema owner bought himself a flash new American car and was mightily chuffed. IFT is still running, in different premises, over thirty years later.

During the year John Birman was putting increasing pressure on me to drop my community arts work and become involved in his conferences for businesses organisations. My contract specifically stated that I was engaged for the community arts programme so, since the director was unwell, I went to see the vice-chancellor. He wouldn't commit himself but offered to pay my expenses home if I didn't like the situation. I was prepared for a fight and I was sure I would win.

Pressure from my wife

Surprisingly, Monica was not keen to back me in this power struggle and kept urging me to quit and find a job somewhere else in Australia. She would keep finding job applications for me. When she discovered that Australia's first School of Sociology was opening at the University of New South Wales in Sydney, I wrote to the new head of department, Professor Sol Encel, who explained that he didn't have a lectureship to offer at this stage but promised that if I became a teaching fellow he would guarantee me a lectureship within two years. This meant a much reduced salary and no tenure. I could undertake a PhD thesis, as the teaching load would be small.

The move to Sydney would involve a big risk. I had been let down by my superiors in WA – could I trust Professor Encel? I knew people who had worked with him at the National University in Canberra and I was assured that he had been active in the Staff Association and was very supportive in staff grievance cases.

Monica was increasing the pressure to move and, even though I loved my job and friends in Perth and was quite looking forward to the struggle for power, I finally agreed to leave. I stayed on to help with the 1967 festival and then in early February we shifted everything to Sydney.

6

Strange goings-on at the University of New South Wales

Change and excitement were in the air when we arrived in Sydney. I was back in the thick of university affairs after my years at Perth as a 'culture vulture', as I was affectionately called by the locals. Monica had found an excellent teaching position and we bought a charming terrace house in Paddington while these were still cheap.

I started on my thesis on art and value orientations. Professor Encel loaded me with classes because I was one of only two members of the new department who actually had a degree in sociology! This was not going to be easy.

Part of the excitement was the news from the United States where youth in general and students in particular were in state of upheaval. All sorts of new and forgotten old ideas were surfacing. I had heard about the theories of Marshall McLuhan and when I got hold of a copy of *The Gutenberg Galaxy* I was knocked sideways by his erudition and stream of insights concerning the relationship between technology and human perception of the world.

Outside our terrace house in Paddington.

I was inspired to start evening sessions and at the end of the year I formed a discussion group we called The Black Guards (pun intended). During the summer vacation I put my nose to the grindstone for my thesis and came across *Homo Ludens* by Johann Huizinga. Once again I was strangely affected by the thesis that high human culture is essentially playful and that puritanical regimes are destructive of civilisation.

Ideas of 'student power' were beginning to affect the Australian students and I felt something should be done to head off the extremists who had begun to take over in the United States. I organised a meeting in the main lecture theatre, which panicked some of the administrative staff, but since it was booked and addressed by myself and more senior academics there was nothing they could do about it. The topic was 'Student Power and Responsibility'. This threw cold water on those student activists who wanted the former without the latter.

ALF

A few weeks later we held a meeting of activists looking for a new way to bring about reform. This adopted my proposal to emphasise love as well as freedom. This synthesis of hippie and radical approaches we called Action for Love and Freedom, with the happy acronym of ALF. I was keen to avoid anything like the pompous and deadly earnest names that middle-class American students and their imitators had chosen for their radical movements. As I was chief catalyst of the Alfs, I was widely known as Grandalf.

The Alfs practised the art of loving their enemies with cheek and obvious delight. We insisted on treating the university as a community of scholars and not just separate groups of teachers, administrators, and students after a meal ticket. The first step was to hold meetings at the Roundhouse and to invite everyone who was interested. The first was a flop because we had left the chairing of the meeting to non-Alfs, who took everything seriously and spent the whole time trying to pass bureaucratic motions.

The Alfs and I took over the next meeting and, having made sure the vice-chancellor, Sir Philip Baxter, would come, advertised it as a revival meeting that would be attended by the deity and accompanying admin angels. I set up an empty chair to represent the invisible spirit of Alf and got a student rock band to provide drum rolls as people approached the chair to speak and to play in between speeches. These events were being covered in the *Australian* and the *Sydney Morning Herald*, who hailed our innovative and non-threatening approach to apathy, boredom, depression and the consequent lower standards of teaching and learning.

The Fun Revolution

In between meetings the Alfs were active in most departments and many of the academic staff supported more fun and more personal involvement in tutorials. Some were held in pubs and I held some in swimming pools and the park. The campus was buzzing with excitement. I began calling this the Fun Revolution. In October I finally put down my thoughts in a short article, 'Soul Power and Funpowder versus Will Power and Gunpowder', which appeared in the student newspaper, *Tharunka*. This became the

Leading the Fun Revolution – I make a speech on campus.

gospel of the Fun Revolution. After careful consultation with academic activists, we produced a short programme of needed university reform we called the Alf Charter.

Some months later, student radicals at Sydney University finally got their act together and began to agitate, copying American student movements in both name and tactics. There was no mention of love or freedom; the word that attracted them was power. Almost daily violent, and occasionally non-violent, confrontations with university, city, state and national authorities made them into heroes of the revolution and they appeared in the papers. Most of this was what Tom Wolfe aptly called 'radical chic'. They saw the Alfs as stupid and 'a distraction from the real issues' – the overthrow of capitalism and its replacement with socialism, despite the fact that, both in material conditions and freedom of expression, our students were better off than those in socialist countries.

'We Shall Not Be Moved'

We, too, had our confrontation, though it wasn't planned. I had been given a room in the Education Department as a reform HQ. Owing to a misunderstood phone message, the administration was told that I had refused to vacate the room for a tutorial group. There was a confrontation in which the Alfs were told bluntly by the VC to leave the premises. For some hours we debated the situation and the Trotskyite element urged the Alfs to stage a sit-in. I reminded the Alfs of our philosophy of love and freedom and recommended that we leave, so we marched out carrying our banners and singing 'We Shall Not Be Moved'.

Impressed with our restraint, the VC said he would arrange a special hut for our use on campus and the student union offered us temporary accommodation in their building. The Alf House, as we named the hut, was an excellent demonstration of the new politics of the absurd and a turning point in revolutionary history.

My old life comes to an end

I was convinced that the fascinating and amazing year of 1968 would be a watershed in history. Huge changes were beginning to take place all over the world.

As my charisma grew, I was becoming more attractive to the opposite sex. At the same time my relationship with Monica, which had begun to take a turn for the worse when she initiated the move from Perth, was in

This photo of me was taken in the Sydney Domain in the exciting summer of 1968. Entitled 'Protest', it won an international photography prize as a symbol of the protest movement. What a pity I wasn't being sincere at the time!

trouble. We lost interest in each other sexually and she regarded my new ideas and activities as pretty pointless.

The result was fairly predictable: I started a light-hearted, playful but physically revitalising affair with a postgraduate from the psychology school. I realised that I had become half of a *folie à deux* and that the great friendship with Monica had kept me from maturing. I also discovered that both of us had been afraid of passion and the risks that follow. At this time my mother came to stay for a short while and she and Monica took off for Mexico for a holiday.

That summer was like a spring for my long repressed love life. I had a brief, intense affair with a beautiful blonde actress and then an even shorter but less intense affair with a Californian girl who, although she had a great sense of humour and was tickled pink by my antics at university, returned home shortly after we met. Was it my lack of commitment that was producing this disastrous effect? Then I met Del, an attractive and very intelligent blonde woman from Sydney University, and was fascinated by her wry sense of humour and association with the bohemian element on her campus.

Lost in thought.

Monica, who returned with my mother shortly afterwards, was becoming suspicious. I hated keeping secrets from her and wanted to find a way to tell her without a mighty explosion. Foolish youth! My mother went home and the row broke out soon afterwards. Alf and the Fun Revolution were bad enough, but other women were the last straw. Monica threw me out.

I swore to her that I would not live in the same house as another woman again and I kept my promise for the next twenty years. My departure from our terrace house was all done in the best possible taste. We organised a last dinner party for our friends and during the evening I left, carrying my bags.

A Hobbit house in Woolloomooloo

I rented a house in Bourke Street, Wooloomooloo, partly because of the magic in the name. I hoped I could attract tenants, especially students who shared the new hippie philosophy of love and sharing but with a special emphasis of my own on fun and imagination. The main house rule was no illegal drugs. Del was a regular visitor.

Every Sunday I would go to the nearby domain with 'the Hobbits' and join the soapbox orators. We gave out thousands of clickers to passers-by in Kings Cross and occasionally put on fur coats and bounced around the Cross on our pogo sticks. I planned to start a small factory to supply garden gnomes to add colour and imagination to the rather sterile campus buildings. For a few weeks in the summer of 1968 I had the time of my life.

Visions

All the unsupervised reading I had done over the years, my experiments and my specialist studies in psychology and the sociology of knowledge began to synthesise in my brain. I felt even more elated than my usual chirpy self. I would wake up having had visions of patterns made up of previously disparate and usually unlinked elements.

Del

 I would then attempt to put words to these abstract patterns in the heightened state that comes when one is successfully orating in front of an audience. I can only call this process a form of superconscious inspiration.

 Using this new analysis I became acutely aware of the dysfunctional nature of male female psycho-sexual relationships. This was the time of the sexual revolution, and all sorts of experiments in relationships were being carried out, especially in the United States. My own thoughts, however, were unlike those I had encountered or read about. I was becoming increasingly aware of the unconscious success of women in inculcating their values into their male children and their mates. This was not a popular conclusion. (See the Appendix for my highly controversial and unpopular theory about men and women.)

7
The making of the University Wizard

As 1968 drew to an end, strings were being pulled behind the scenes. My professor, a socialist, had not been amused by the Fun Revolution, which had set the campus ablaze with mirth. I was also busy travelling to other campuses spreading the good news. His supervision of my thesis was most unsatisfactory. I was given only a few minutes of his time every six months or so and I had a very heavy teaching load in addition to my involvement in university affairs.

I also wanted to revise my thesis in line with my experiences in resolving tension through absurd behaviour as a kind of positive feedback where the underdog teaches the overdog in order to reveal mutual interests. Since this would involve a major departure from the original topic, I wrote to the professor, seeking his agreement to the changes. As I received no reply I became concerned and wrote to the Higher Degrees Committee.

Then came the death blow. At the very end of 1968 I received a letter from the committee stating baldly that my thesis was terminated owing to 'insufficient progress'. Since my teaching fellowship was dependent on my advancing my thesis I was dismissed. A few weeks later I heard that Sydney University no longer needed my services as a tutor for a special course in recent developments in urban civilisation planned earlier as a follow-on to my lectures on Marshall McLuhan at the Free University.

Hitting rock bottom

I had already given up my security and comfort as a husband and house owner to take part in the great adventure of the late 1960s. My career was as dead as my marriage and my old friends believed I had gone mad. There had been no communication with my professor: my letters remained unanswered and he was almost impossible to get hold of. (I was later told that both he and his wife were involved in my dismissal.)

I had become the key figure in preventing both the mindless violence of the Trotskyite radicals and the 'dropping out' alternative of the sex, drugs and rock and roll crowd. The students were stunned and academics active in the reform movement urged me to sue the university for breach of contract. At the same time, a very interesting article appeared in *Pol* magazine, reporting my fate and likening me to the Pied Piper betrayed by the authorities he had successfully helped, and an ABC documentary in the excellent 'Special Project' series was being made about the Hobbit House and our friends around Kings Cross and the university. During the filming of a beach battle between the Pythagoreans and the Heraclitans I almost drowned in a rip at Bondi. Luckily I was wearing a fur coat under my suit of armour, which provided buoyancy.

After six months it was obvious that I had failed to stop drugs coming into the Hobbit House and most of my tenants began to show the signs of addiction. They couldn't (or wouldn't) pay the rent, they lost their sense of fun, they started to hang around the house all day and unsavoury types began to call round. I closed the house down and, having nowhere else to go, was forced to share a room with Del.

I had lost everything. How could things get worse? They could, and did. But first I had to rebuild my life.

Déjà vu

Before the next university year started I went to see the vice-chancellor about my situation. He was shocked to find out that I had given up a tenured lectureship in WA for a promise by Professor Encel that I would be reappointed in a year or two at the latest and that I had all the time in the world to complete my thesis. Academic appointments had to go to the professorial board and be ratified by the University Council. I had been misled.

I had a strong feeling of *déjà vu*. Only two years earlier I had been standing in the WA vice-chancellor's office as the result of being let down by the head of my department. The Sydney VC even came up with the same offer: the university would pay to return me and my effects to Britain!

The turning point

This time I was not going to run away and leave my enemies in possession of the field. I proposed that I stay on campus as a catalyst for new ideas for people with rigid personalities and for gentler techniques to transform rigid structures. I never wanted to be under the control of a professor again. I had

had enough. I preferred to trust the VC's word of honour rather than an academic contract. I would need a humble honorarium for the first year until I had learnt how to finance myself.

Although I was a junior academic who had been hell-raising at the university (in a friendly way), I could see that he regarded me with a great deal of respect. This was not something I was used to. He went pale, however, when I explained that I needed a special title to clearly distinguish my activities from those of an academic, politician, social worker or priest. I wanted to become the official 'wizard' of the university – under his overall supervision, of course. Since he was the most senior vice-chancellor in Australia, and later became chairman of the Atomic Energy Commission, he had enough self-esteem to ignore the inevitable mockery of the academic fraternity and, with a chuckle, agreed to give it a go. He made one proviso, with which I wholeheartedly agreed: the student union must meet in a plenary session to vote for the proposal and must share the costs of the honorarium 50/50 with the university administration.

Have your worst suspicions confirmed

Once the proposal became known the puritanical radicals went berserk and made all sorts of accusations about my sanity and motives and those of the VC. I had to think of a way to outsmart their slander campaign.

I put on a special performance before the student body the day of the meeting, which I called *Have Your Worst Suspicions Confirmed (a paranoiac psychodrama)*. The advertisements took the form of a questionnaire that gave students the opportunity to tick which of two opposing statements they agreed with. These included: 'Channell is the VC's stooge/The VC is Channell's stooge', 'Channell is a fool/Channell is making fools of us all', 'Channell is a sex maniac/Channell is sexually frustrated', etc.

During the performance I wore my black leather jacket and peaked radical's hat as a trendy young academic and mocked the whole proposal of the university appointing a wizard as a distraction from genuine attempts to change the world. Then I put on my gown and pointed hat to mock the trendy hypocritical and bad-mannered young radical, who was all talk, saw nothing wrong with tyrants like Stalin or Mao and behaved heartlessly towards his colleagues and his students.

It was a knockout. My enemies were stunned that I could so successfully present what was going on in their nasty little minds. That evening the student body voted unanimously for the proposal with one abstention, the sports officer. I was on my way again.

A wizard at the court of the Vice-Chancellor

I wish I had the space to describe the extraordinary events of 1969 when the University of New South Wales became the most exciting university in Australia. During the year my visits to other universities were spectacularly successful. I became a good friend of a local Yankee DJ and postgraduate student who put on Mad Mel's Giant Stirs, a series of stunning crowd spectacles held under the pylon of the Harbour Bridge, in a city park and on Bondi Beach, in which I featured.

In July came the spiritual high point of the year. A few days after Prince Charles was invested, I 'invested' the new VC, Sir Rupert Myers, as 'Prince of New South Wales'. Following the ceremonies, the day was declared to be

I perform at the third of Mad Mel's Giant Stirs.

Fun Day and a mob of students invaded the city; there were no unpleasant incidents.

Shortly after this I produced and directed *At Last the 1848 Student Power Show* in the Roundhouse. In this form of living theatre, the VC played the part of the VC, the student president the part of the student president and so on. As they entered, the students themselves were allocated student power faction labels and placed strategically. I played the part of a junior academic who, horrified by growing intolerance, hostility and violence on the campus, turned into a wizard during the first part and broke the escalating violence with a spell. The second part was pure late 1960s psychedelia, performed in the dark with strobes, body paint and lightly clad dancers. In the third part, as master of ceremonies, I demolished the boundary between performers and audience. Given clickers, toy trumpets and kazoos, the audience began to make an unholy din. A spotlight revealed, in the dome of the Roundhouse, a gigantic inflated figure. 'Eat the body of God!' I shouted. The figure descended and was torn apart by the liberated audience. Inside the figure were sweets that were quickly consumed and everybody danced for joy. We had become 'The University that Swings', as the *Sydney Morning Herald* put it at the time.

Peasant power during the Jun Revolution in the streets of Sydney, 1969.

The dictatorship

In September I went to Geneva on behalf of the World University Service and obtained their backing for the Fun Revolution in Australia and New Zealand.

While I was away there was a sneaky bureaucratic takeover of the student union by a group of traditional radicals. The permanent staff were resigning, the funds were misappropriated and morale was at an all-time low. After listening to endless petty mutual recriminations at a special general meeting of the student body, I proposed that I be elected Dictator of the Student Union until the end of the year (two weeks away). I pledged to restore morale among the staff and to raise funds to replenish the empty treasury.

At a time when the mere mention of the word wizard would cause radicals to froth at the mouth, this proposal was like asking a church council to vote for the Antichrist. The same people who had bullied the staff and students alike during their short regime opposed the motion with so much passion that they were almost incoherent with rage. This was what finally decided the students to vote in favour of the amazing motion.

I had achieved another unbelievable triumph for the Fun Revolution – not only the first man in history to be appointed a university wizard by a university administration, but also the first man ever appointed dictator of a student union. I donned a suitable new uniform and held daily 'Kensington rallies', surrounded by uniformed henchmen and safely out of reach of the barrage of missiles. The student 'peasants' were taxed and got a lapel button as a receipt. Those who wouldn't pay were executed by 'pie kill' (a shaving cream pie in the face).

As dictator, I address a rally.

I changed my title to 'Tyrant' as it had a more dramatic ring and put a well-endowed female 'Tyrantess' in my place for a few days so she could model the new 'Dictatorship of the University of New South Wales' T-shirts, which raised money for the impoverished student union. Another cunning plan to raise money was that most of the rotten fruit thrown at us during the rallies was sold to the peasants by henchmen in mufti. I even encouraged my own opposition, the Black Spider, whose slogan was 'Death to All Tyrants', equipped him with a spider costume and gave him flares to let off on the top of the highest buildings while he defied me during rally speeches.

Parallel universes

At the same time as I was dictator I was standing as a democratic candidate in the Australian federal elections for the seat of Sydney Central with the slogan 'Pop a Wizard into Parliament'. I had no money to campaign with but got a surprising number of votes.

On the final day of the dictatorship I went mad with power and led a huge procession up the campus to the chancellory and shouted out that I was no longer content to be merely the students' dictator. I wanted to replace the VC and become the Dictator of the University. To everyone's horror, the VC came out on his balcony and ordered me to his office.

My henchmen went pale and the student mob started muttering that I'd gone too far this time. I marched confidently into the building. Security staff quickly locked the doors in case others followed me in. I came out on to the balcony where, to my surprise, Sir Rupert swiftly wrapped me in red tape, threw away the Alf Charter I was carrying and opened his jacket to reveal he was wearing . . . a dictatorship T-shirt! My henchmen cried out 'Hail Rupert' and Max Merritt and the Meteors played in the sunshine. The university year was over. What a finale for 1969.

Wizard of the World University Service

During that summer the World University Service of Australasia held its AGM. Their endorsement of me as a wizard who raised fun and funds on campuses was greeted with enthusiasm and the director set up the structure to enable Del (my hon. sec.) and me to start travelling around the universities with our own show on a regular basis. I was now the Wizard of the World University Service of Australasia.

In addition a motion was passed that I be considered a 'living work of art', as I had cut myself free from any identity other than that of the Wizard

In dictator mode, accompanied by the 'Tyrantess'.

since Ian Brackenbury Channell had died to the world. I had allowed all his documentation to expire (note the change in pronouns): no driving licence, no passport, no welfare ID, no bank accounts or personal property other than the books and costumes that were the tools of my trade. Ian Channell had legally expired and his body was taken over by the daemon of a wizard. As the Wizard I was obviously a fictional character. No one, including me, believed that wizards were real in a world run by businessmen, accountants, physicists and psychiatrists. It was all done for fun, and with an eye to the future.

The Immorality Show

In March 1970 I made my last appearance at the University of New South Wales in a bizarre synthesis of a medieval PhD thesis and pantomime – a series of three lecture/performances of *The Immorality Show*. (The VC gave me free use of the main university lecture theatre.) Del and I and the henchmen, using a portable Ark of the Covenant that also served as a sedan chair, a four-poster bed and a Punch and Judy theatre, traced the history of mankind from the creation of Adam to the death of God. At the end of the final performance I left the stage and the university to begin acting in a real-life drama that I called 'The Immortality Show'.

8

The University Wizard
bites the dust

In April 1970 Del and I set off on our World University Service tour of
Australian campuses, first Melbourne and then Perth. Trouble had been brewing between us for some months. In Perth, for no reason I could understand, she became aggressively hostile, refused to co-operate, and insisted
on going on ahead to Adelaide. When I got to Adelaide she was extremely
depressed and so negative that I had to leave and press on to my next
appearance in Tasmania.

Down and out in Melbourne

When I finally got back to Melbourne I found that the head office of WUS
had been moved and none of my urgent letters to the director, Brendon
O'Dwyer, were answered. I was devastated. What on earth could I do? I had
trusted the WUS people, whom I regarded as personal friends, and had cut
all my contractual links with the institutional world to operate through my
new philosophy of love and freedom. Trust was now a key element in my life
and without any explanation, and for no reason I could find, I had lost not
only Del but all my support from the WUS.

With no money, no job and no friends and, even worse, no explanation
of how or why this could have happened, I rented a cheap room near Melbourne University and lived on fried rice at the university caf. I wrote to Del
for a few weeks, but her replies were almost incomprehensible. All I could
gather was that she wanted to be left alone in her beloved Adelaide.

In 1971 I approached Anna Carmody, the activities officer of Melbourne
University Union, with a proposal that I become their official Wizard (unpaid), with the associated functions of Living Work of Art, Shaman and
Cosmologer, and charged with organising WUS events on the campus. The
council agreed.

I had underestimated the hatred that the Fun Revolution would gener-

The Wizard as martyr.

ate. Someone had certainly nobbled WUS and I was pretty sure that Del had been turned against me. There were only two possible courses of action: I could go back into my pre-1968 shell and escape into anarchistic back-packing, or I could carry on, but only after more careful thought and planning.

The fun I had shared with so many people and the amazing insights I had gained over the past two years made it possible to bear all the personal betrayals and openly expressed hatred of the increasingly powerful serious revolutionaries. Before starting again at Melbourne University I needed a more foolproof 'model of reality' before I could trust anyone again so fully. It was also clear that love and trust had to be given in such a way that one was not destroyed if these were betrayed.

I create my own universe and live in it

While I was in Perth someone pointed out to me that there was no proof that the universe was outside the Earth's surface. According to relativity theory, the Earth could be a kind of 'hole in infinite matter' with the observable universe inside it. What a revelation! I wasn't even obliged to take the *physical* universe seriously any more. There were considerable advantages to the inside-out model, apart from upsetting the crazy materialists who believe they are essentially ghostly observers of a 'real' universe outside them.

The Department of Levity

This is not the place to set out the elaborate cosmology I created while at Melbourne University. In 1972 I was able to persuade the VC to let me have the use of the beautiful old Pathology Lecture Theatre as a base for teaching and designing the new reality. I named the new department the Department of Levity to put off both credulous new-age trendies and materialists, who were obsessed with gravity in all its forms. I gave several courses on cosmology and had the invaluable help of a physicist, Dr Derek Banks, in fitting a physical base to my biological, behavioural, psychological, social and cultural superstructure.

Monica, back in Britain, had sent me money from the sale of our house and effects, and I used some of this to send copies of my outline to universities in Europe and the United States to let them know what I was doing; good science depends on sharing one's findings and insights, not hoarding them, like commercial firms or weapons designers, to make a killing later. As I expected, I received absolutely no response. I had altered their paradigm far too much. My new cosmology was, in any case, existential, evolving and ultimately subjective and designed primarily for my own use.

My body donated to the art gallery

In 1972 the university union approached the director of the National Gallery of Victoria with the offer of my living body – I was now a fictional character on regular exhibition to the public – to add to their collection of dead works of art. As a self-maintaining conceptual art form, I would require neither a government grant nor any financial support from the gallery. The director, Eric Westbrook, gave the idea his full support.

The Dirtiest Show on Earth

This show, backed by a maverick entrepreneur and staged in a wrestling arena, was a celebration of dirt. I entered in a bath carried by my henchmen through the audience. On stage, still in my bath, I was accompanied by a band playing 'My Baby Has Gorn Down the Plug'ole' until I was seized by a vision of doom. 'Omo sapiens is drowning in his own suds' – the words haunted me: there was a general obsession with cleanliness, both physical

Watched by dollybirds, I orate on a soapbox outside the National Gallery of Victoria, to which my body was offered as a living work of art.

and mental, and the solution was to learn to love dirt again. Mud was poured over me as the band played 'Mud, Mud, Glorious Mud' and I arose in my filthy state as the 'Messiah of the Gutters'.

Trying to get high at a rock festival

I was also involved in the first rock festivals in Victoria. The biggest and most successful, at Sunbury, was attended by 100,000 raving supporters of the counter-culture. I will never forget the response when I appeared on the stage in a bird-man costume to announce that I would be able to fly if only the huge audience had faith in me rather than in God or nature. Alas, they had no faith but I defied them and leapt out of a tree. I flapped like mad but didn't get very far before plummeting; I had taken the precaution of choosing a tree overhanging a river!

My first experiment with slavery for women

With my cosmology to guide and protect me, I embarked on my first attempt to realise my new plan for improving the existing male/female relationship system. In 1971–72, within a few months of each other, three

Wizard with wings: in my bird-man costume at the Sunbury rock festival, 1972.

young women who showed signs of interest in me were prepared to take on the role of romantic slaves, with the right to leave at any time. I gave each of them a set of typed notes and references to psychological, ethological and anthropological texts, on how I would relate to them so that they could not later complain or try to change the rules.

One of them took too much pot and soon left. Another, who was a bright girl with a job and a car, and not a university student (thank God), would have stuck to it longer but her mother went berserk and made her leave.

Alice in Wonderland

The third and final young woman to take on the role was Alison, a classics student and devout Roman Catholic. I was worried that this unspoilt and rather serious young woman could lose more than she might gain from such an experimental relationship. The other girls did not have her stable and ethical background. I tried to put her off.

For months Alice (as I called her) would drop in to the terrace house I lived in near the university with students and junior academics. She was interested in my ideas and even read some of the books I recommended. I

The Wizard being admired by Alice.

71

was stunned! I warned her that although she had never hated anyone in her life she would become consumed with jealousy if she became a slave. Alison was interested in becoming a nun but unfortunately she was just as interested in men, though she was choosy and spent some time checking me out before she made her move.

Within a few days she was transformed from a sweet young thing into a jealous tigress. Unlike the others, Alice had a mind of her own and incredible tenacity. She was determined to make the relationship work and was by now deeply in love with me, whatever the cost. By the end of a year she was left in possession of the field but I didn't change the rules of limited interaction, living apart and remaining independent of each other to maximise trust.

Sending myself up in every sense of the word

With intense excitement, I finished constructing the bare bones of my cosmology in 1973. Its ultimately subjective and personal nature was so different from both modern cosmology and traditional religious cosmologies that I named it the Postmodern Cosmology. (The word 'postmodern' is now common but usually indicates the same exhausted modern ideas disguised by being overlaid with garish architectural or verbal decoration.)

The only way I could make sure it was an open-ended system was to include the potential for the shaman-cosmologer himself, and possibly others, to defy all forms of gravity and vanish while ascending into the centre of the new universe. This clearly avoided the irrational obsession with immortality that accompanies the 'death wish'. I realised, however, that it was not going to improve the chances of any religious or secular intellectuals being interested in my cosmology.

Single-handedly stopping the revolution

During my three years at Melbourne University I was able to outmanoeuvre all attempts to hold snap meetings of the student body at which they would be bombarded with demagoguery and then persuaded to vote for an 'occupation' of the administration building. I would use my powerful skills as a demagogue to sway the masses away from violent action to overthrow the system. Instead I offered sensible direct-action methods to achieve reforms on the campus itself. No one really wanted reform: it was revolution or nothing, and so they got nothing.

I was now the Antichrist of student politics, hissed at wherever I went and surrounded by empty seats whenever I ate in the student caf. A few students who had attended my lectures in cosmology stuck with me, and they are still friends today. They backed me in my election campaigns in Kooyong and helped run a stall in the union foyer. The stalls around us were for fundamentalist Christians and Zionists, Trotskyite Marxists, feminist Marxists, marijuana law liberalisation and birth control. The music outside was rock and roll. Our stall was devoted to the British monarchy, postmodern cosmology, men's liberation and British Israel. We always wore dress suits and played imperial brass band music on a wind-up gramophone. The student 'heavies' hated it, but all they could do was shout 'fascist' and occasionally knock over the stall, all of which we bore with Christian patience.

Alf's Imperial Army

Derek Banks, my collaborator in cosmology construction, was a member of the student Pacifist Society. When this was taken over by the revolutionaries and voted money to the Viet Cong, this was the last straw. Peace had now become a word that really meant war against capitalist imperialism. Shades of *1984*!

I decided I could revive the old Alf henchmen idea and formed Alf's Imperial Army, a body of students who dressed in white druidic robes and

Grandalf with the general staff of Alf's Imperial Army.

declared war an any anti-imperialists who wanted a battle. We drew up rules of warfare so no one would get hurt. When we said 'imperialist war' we meant playful peace! Battles took place almost weekly on the 'concrete lawn' between the student and university administration buildings and there was flour and water everywhere. The serious anti-imperialists wouldn't fight with us because we weren't violent but fortunately other groups, such as the engineers, were only too happy to oblige, though we were often greatly out-numbered.

The end of the serious revolution

Meanwhile a great change was coming over the millennarian radical students in Melbourne. Off came the Che Guevara hats and Mao badges and they got behind the Labor Party and Gough Whitlam, their new messiah. They even used student funds without student approval to help his campaign and I was in big trouble for daring to criticise. Labor won the 1972 federal election, in which I stood as a monarchist candidate in Kooyong and got another surprisingly good result. Several attempts were made to scare me away and even to make the union council fire me for no reason, but luckily Anna Carmody did not respond to emotional blackmail.

It was time to go but I did not leave without a parting shot. I had persuaded the Activities Committee to publish my *Nonsense Almanac*, a collection of my various writings, and to distribute them free to the students. It was a great hit.

Shortly afterwards I left Australia for Christchurch, New Zealand, where I would have to start from the bottom all over again. My devoted Alice left her family and the city she loved so much to follow me on this last enterprise.

9

A postmodern prophet in Christchurch

Ian Brackenbury Channell had been killed off by a combination of jealous wife and petty-minded professor. The Wizard of the Universities had been killed off by panicking administrators and puritanical student radicals. Could I resurrect myself for a third time, away from the world of materialistic career intellectuals?

New Zealand, especially the South Island, had been in my thoughts for some years as a country small, sane and British enough to support a sceptical and witty nonconformist. It was obvious that Australia was too urbanised, too serious and too Americanised to put up with me.

Christchurch in 1974 was a sleepy, extremely conservative English-style cathedral town in the South Island. The citizens could be roused to political action only by infringements in the parks or plans for demolishing old and respected buildings. Church fêtes, rugby football, garden shows, choral singing and Anglicanism made up the pervasive cultural ambience. I had visited the city the year before and recognised that the local people were both very hospitable and capable of coping with visitors from other cultures.

I also observed that Cathedral Square was an excellent place for a prophet, both because of its dramatic location in front of the Anglican cathedral and its excellent acoustics. The only snag appeared to be the loutish behaviour of the Christian fundamentalists who harassed passers-by with their unspeakable heresies, and the bikies who lounged about accosting all and sundry with foul language.

The medium is the message

In Melbourne I had written to the Anglican church authorities asking them to examine my claim to be a prophet. Since I received no acknowledgement of my letter, I assumed that the church didn't care either way about my mission.

The arrival of the Prophet on 17 September 1974, beginning a twenty-four-year career of oratory in Christchurch's Cathedral Square, was a momentous event. Wearing a brown, animal-skin-like costume, I began addressing the astonished locals in the recently improved Square on such topics as the evils of usury, the need for an established state religion, the necessity for men to inspire obedience in their wives and the dangers of secularisation, especially multicultural, Disney Americanisation.

I had taken the trouble to visit the responsible city council authorities to show them my letters of introduction from the University of Melbourne, as Wizard, Shaman and Living Work of Art. I also provided documentary evidence of my friendly relationship with the Melbourne City Council, who had granted me permission to speak regularly in their rather noisy and cluttered city square. I also called into the police station to present my credentials and to inform them of my intention to speak regularly in the Square. They advised me to 'play it by ear'.

But Mr A. P. Milthorpe, the council's chief health inspector, was not impressed and warned me I would be arrested if I tried to speak. I was informed that there was a by-law that forbade 'speaking or praying out loud' in Cathedral Square. He was obdurate; I informed him that this decision would lead to a head-on conflict and that I was an inspired opponent.

Maiden speech violated

A group of drunken louts threw a couple of dozen eggs at me during my maiden speech (I dodged them all successfully except one thrown from behind) and I was apprehended by the police. I finally convinced them that they were acting rather strangely by arresting the victim rather than the perpetrators of the crime, so they released me without charge and arrested two furiously fighting women instead. This was the last time anyone forcibly prevented the Prophet from speaking in Cathedral Square, but not from lack of trying.

The next day a police inspector interrupted my speech on the importance of the British monarchy and the Anglican church to inform me that I was contravening a by-law: I must obtain a permit from the council to speak in Cathedral Square itself. I promised I would do this. I also promised the crowd that I would speak again the next day.

In John the Baptist guise, the Prophet addresses his audience in Cathedral Square and assists the police with their inquiries.

An arresting orator

Meanwhile the numbers of curious locals coming to hear me speak were growing steadily, especially since the likelihood of a confrontation with the city-council bureaucracy had been reported on the front page of the morning newspaper, *The Press*.

The next day the council refused me a permit to speak. Once again I committed the crime of 'speaking out loud' in Cathedral Square. Mr M. W. Atkinson, the assistant town clerk, informed *The Press* that I was an obvious troublemaker, but said that the council was prepared to 'reconsider' granting me a permit 'at a later date'. I was warned that the next day, however, that I would be arrested if I persisted.

The next day I moved closer to the cathedral, where the fundamentalists regularly gathered. I began to explain that, according to the Bible, the British people were the Ten Lost Tribes of Israel and that the Queen was descended from the House of David. I was therefore dedicated to converting their brothers the Jews to the Anglican faith and to bringing the renegade republican American Episcopalians back to the British Crown and Empire.

I was interrupted by the dean, Michael Underhill, who had been warned by the council that I would speak there and that he should call the police. The dean, a delightful man who later became a friend, unwisely followed this advice and the police accused me of trespassing. He did, though, tell *The Press* that I was very polite and had given him documentation outlining my position as a postmodern prophet *vis-à-vis* the modern church.

All this took place on Friday. On Saturday, attired in a grass skirt and Union Jack shirt, I went to the Square and cast an elaborate spell on the assistant town clerk for his slanderous remarks about my being a provoker of violence – to bind up his bowels for a week. He took the trouble to assure *The Press* later that there were no signs of the spell working.

Silence, gentlemen, please

Monday came and the crowds and city council officials were awaiting the Prophet's next move. I appeared in frockcoat and top hat, carrying a silver-topped cane. Standing on a soapbox, decorated with a tea tray bearing the Queen's head, and carrying a sign saying 'Silence! No speaking or praying out loud in Cathedral Square . . . by order Christchurch City Council', I began my speech. My lips moved and my hands gesticulated wildly, but not a sound came forth. The crowd, thoroughly onside, began heckling in the same manner. The performance made the front page of *The Press* next day.

The Prophet boxes clever

On Tuesday a large cardboard box was carried into the Square and placed at the top of the steps by some of the Prophet's henchmen, dressed in white gowns. The box was labelled, 'To Cathedral Square, Christchurch, from Heaven'. Smoke issued from inside, accompanied by the sound of fireworks, a bugle sounded and a small Union Jack emerged from a hole in the top. From inside the box I addressed the crowd in somewhat muffled tones. A youth pushed the box over and was thrust away by the loyal henchmen, who righted the box not only on this occasion but whenever I got too carried away by my oratory to maintain the precarious balance required.

Prophet offers services to council

In late September I wrote a four-page letter to the council offering my services and following up my first prophecy (printed in the local magazine, *Time Off*) concerning the need to balance logic, love and levity. I emphasised my skill in confounding heretics, such as those who had been holding forth outside the cathedral doors for years, and offered to attack modern ideas in my unique postmodern fashion and 'to make occasional forays on behalf of the Christchurch City Council into that sink of iniquity and seething nest of heresy, the University of Canterbury'. For payment I required only help in typing and publishing and co-operation in finding food and accommodation for my humble needs. I informed them that my time might be limited as I was attempting to ascend on 4 December that year.

A few days later I wrote again to the council, supplying evidence of my experience at Melbourne University as head of the Department of Levity. I asked if they would like me to give similar free lectures on cosmology in Christchurch.

My third and final approach to the council was to ask if they would accept my offer to exhibit myself (clothed of course) 'as a free aesthetic entertainment for the citizens of Christchurch'. This time I supplied documents showing that the director of the National Gallery of Victoria had recognised my unique qualities as a living work of art.

The council wrote back rejecting my offers on the grounds that 'the Municipal Corporations Act did not appear to cover the type of activities' I proposed. I examined the act and found that the council was authorised and expected to provide cultural stimulation for the ratepayers. This they had singularly failed to do for those whose tastes did not extend to expensive concerts or art galleries.

10

The Wizard's war with the council

Tension was rising as the council 'suits' became ever more determined to crush the upstart prophet/wizard/cosmologer/living work of art. In particular Councillor Newton Dodge, a fundamentalist and chairman of the Health Committee, which controlled the Square, let it be known that the Wizard had been given his final warning.

Each day the crowds came to see what would happen, and each day the master did not disappoint them. Wearing Middle Eastern costume, I spoke in tongues for an hour; I gave a fine speech in fluent French; I spoke in a gas mask; I wrote on a blackboard. The bureaucrats didn't dare make a move as I demonstrated the power of logic, love and levity to individuals seriously lacking in all three departments.

Letters swamped the local newspapers, most of them supporting my spiritual revitalisation of a moribund city centre. Those opposing me were so vindictive, untrue and stupid that they helped my cause even more than those who praised me.

God saves the Wizard

One of the letter writers was highly critical of the cathedral authorities' decision to have me threatened with arrest if I spoke on their ground. The writer pointed out that, in the past, the church had allowed rabble-rousing extreme left-wingers the right to speak on their land. How could they justify their persecution of a witty and humorous supporter of God, Queen and Empire?

The dean, quoted in the *Press* as saying that he called the police 'to back up the City Council', went on to say that 'the Wizard was a harmless thing . . . but he was breaking by-laws . . . He left me with a pile of pamphlets, one of which indicated he is British Israelite.' Presumably this was worse to the Anglican establishment than being a republican agnostic or atheistical Communist!

This was what I had been waiting for. Having established the exact point where God's and the people's territories met, I stood on God's side and addressed the crowds in the Square; they could not be stopped from listening on council land.

Trapped on top of the world

Having failed to find a boat to take me to Antipodes Island in time for the moment of my ascension into heaven, I realised I was trapped in the world of illusions and decided to be content with inverting the Earth so that at least I was on top rather than down under. I printed hundreds of South Up Maps showing New Zealand in the centre and at the top. These proved more popular with overseas tourists (who were flocking to the Square to see the living legend) than with the locals.

I strike a typical pose outside the cathedral.

Victory for God and the Wizard

The cathedral authorities did not call the police again. The weather was wonderful and the crowds came. They could make up their own minds about the value of what their Prophet exemplified in his lifestyle and communicated with his brilliant oratory. My enemies in high places could only gnash their teeth in fury and wait for me to make a mistake or go away and leave them alone. Fat chance!

Proclamation nailed to cathedral doors

The Press had revealed that the dean and chapter were involved in negotiations with the city bureaucrats to transfer control of the cathedral grounds to the council. Enraged at this betrayal of sacred land to the malevolent secular authorities, I girded my loins and hastened to the Square, where I delivered a powerful sermon on the need for an established church to protect the citizens from the unfettered power of the state. Then, accompanied by a crowd, I strode over to the cathedral.

I nail my prophetic proclamation to the doors of the cathedral.

Crying out that I was about to damage cathedral property with four drawing pins, I affixed the following prophetic proclamation to the main doors: 'It is neither The Will of God nor The Will of The People that the Cathedral authorities should voluntarily place the Christchurch Cathedral precincts under the abominable by-laws of the C.C.C. By order . . . The Prophet of Christchurch.' Unfortunately a young man, apparently possessed by evil spirits and showing signs of mental instability, tore down the beautiful document shortly afterwards muttering, 'Rubbish, a load of rubbish!'

In December, first the *Star* and then *The Press* wrote editorials praising the Wizard's impact on the city. There was mention, for example, of my 'rare brand of personality, imagination and intuition' and the point was made that a licensed wizard would 'be a rare adornment for a city'.

Newton Dodge breaks the Eighth Commandment

The whole city was arguing about the Wizard. The papers were full of letters and every pub was debating the issue. But Councillor Newton Dodge was far from happy. A few days after the supportive editorials he told *The Press* that he had had complaints about abusive and insulting language from the Wizard. 'He is offensive, and has even asked in writing to be appointed the Prophet of Christchurch, be paid a salary and be given board and lodging.' Fortunately my application to the council had been in writing, and copies had been given to the newspapers and radio stations. Councillor Dodge's words could easily be shown to be the smear tactics of a desperate man.

To maintain purity and freedom from the demands of Mammon I had taken great care to avoid being on anyone's payroll for several years. I had offered my services to the council free and had simply sought their assistance in finding board and lodging, as I was a stranger in a strange land. 'I could take Councillor Dodge to court,' I told *The Press*, 'and I am certain I would win my case. However, as I am a prophet and not a politician, I will leave it to God to punish Councillor Dodge for breaking the Eighth Commandment so blatantly. May God have mercy on his soul.'

I rarely use bad, and never obscene, language. Anyone who has any acquaintance with the Bible will know that prophets regularly used strong language when confronted with hypocrisy or decadence. I suspected that the 'foul language' that so shocked Councillor Dodge was my use of the word 'bullshit'.

The next day outside the cathedral I cast a spell to reduce the size of Councillor Dodge's head. I inflated a balloon with his face painted on it and, after a lengthy tirade, pricked it.

The highlight of the amazingly stupid council debate that followed was Newton Dodge's repeated assertion, in a rather Pecksniffian manner, that his head had not grown any smaller – he had measured it!

The upshot was that I could stay in the Square until February, when the matter would be reviewed. Since there was no way they could prevent me from speaking on cathedral land, this was no great concession. I suspected that the Anglican authorities would not go out of their way to please Councillor Dodge, who made no secret of his dislike of orthodox religion. The Prophet was inspired to write a short poem for *The Press*:

> *Jesus loves you, Newton D,*
> *Even though you are a B.*
> *B is for Baptist, but not for me.*
> *For I'm the Prophet of the C of E.*

The Prophet's mother arrives

All this time I had been sending my seventy-one-year-old mother in England copies of the newspaper coverage of my hilarious struggles with church and state. She was rather bored with her life in a small town in East Anglia so came to Christchurch for an extended visit. A couple of years after returning home she decided to sell her house and join me in New Zealand.

During the fifteen years remaining to her she had the time of her life here. She was feted wherever she went as the 'Wizard's Mum'. Everyone wanted to know what sort of child I had been. She had to confess that I wasn't much different. I was just a lot smarter now. We appeared together at many functions and people were amazed at her humour and vitality.

Council surrenders, speakers' corner set up

The sub-committee set up to report on the best use of Cathedral Square were in favour of a livelier Square, and even recommended a speakers' corner in the area where I had been holding forth. On Monday 17 February 1975 the Christchurch City Council meeting endorsed their proposal. The Prophet's Holy War was over.

Things were beginning to look up. I was able to speak in Cathedral Square. Maybe now the council would consider my proposals to be their official prophet, cosmologer and living work of art. This did not prove so easy.

That summer season was very successful as the word got round that I

With my mother at a peace rally in Cathedral Square.

LARRY ROSS

was a stimulating and original speaker. The crowds were spellbound by my fluency and the extraordinary range and originality of my views on important topics. What appealed most of all was my total lack of sincerity and frank admission that I spoke partly because I enjoyed the sound of my own voice and partly because, if I stopped speaking, I would have to listen to far inferior ideas.

The Devil and the Bible Lady

I was soon targeted by the fundamentalists, who, along with the gangs, regarded Cathedral Square as their territory. The most notorious of all was Renée Stanton, already notorious for pestering all the radio talkback programmes. She had been given the name the 'Bible Lady' by well-known local broadcaster John Blumsky.

She devoted the next fifteen years of her life to stopping me from speaking. Initially she attempted to get the council to do it, claiming I was both obscene and a blasphemer, but they had already tried and failed. She also approached feminist organisations, claiming I was insulting women. This was certainly true, but since I also insulted men (and even myself), I could not easily be labelled a sexist. She also claimed I was anti-Jewish. She was the last person to claim this, since she was herself a Jew who had converted. I think it was my claim that the British are the Ten Lost Tribes of Israel that sent her up the wall.

Then she decided to come into the Square each day and make it impossible for me to be heard. She would stand right in front of me and play a violin to drown out my speech. I spoke from my ladder and she played and spoke from her ladder. If she had been a trombonist she might have succeeded.

I am by nature tolerant and easy-going and, like most serious people, she was short-tempered and fanatical. I would tease her to the point of striking me with her violin bow and she once damaged it in the process. This was not at all what she wanted. She hoped that my patience would snap and that I would lash out at her. Then she could call the police and my career as a speaker would be over. When she struck me I didn't call the police but forgave her as a true Christian. Ho! Ho!

She did call the police on two occasions. Once, when she was being particularly obnoxious, one of my disciples, Brother Tony, clad in a white shift and wearing roller skates, squirted her with a water pistol loaded with holy water. We knew that devils and heretics are terrified of holy water. She went berserk and reported him. The police called at his house and told him to hold out his hand. They said 'naughty boy' and smacked his wrist.

The other time was when I was 'blessing' my crowd with a large plastic hammer that squeaks on impact. I have blessed thousands in this way. I get children to form a queue and when they reach me they kneel down to receive my blessing. Many would now have children themselves, but they still remember that marvellous occasion in their childhood. I even blessed my mother, who often hid at the back of the crowd to enjoy the show. (She did not want me to spot her lest I should launch into a speech on how she oppressed me as a boy and exploited me as cheap child labour.) I finally blessed the Bible Lady, who complained of assault and a pain in her head, and went off to fetch the police. My mother and I accompanied her to the police station where I demonstrated how painless the process was by blessing all the police and my mother, who was at least ten years older than Renée. The police found it hard to keep their faces straight as they advised me not to bless her again unless she asked me to.

The Bible Lady and I battle it out in the Square.

86

DECLARATION ᵒꜰ WAR

Be it known throughout the Canterbury Region

THAT

having declined even to attempt to fulfil the conditions clearly put forward in the ULTIMATUM of October 31st 1975 of the Christian Era

A STATE OF WAR

now exists between The Peoples' Representatives known as

THE CHRISTCHURCH CITY COUNCIL

and The Peoples' champion against the gloom and bureaucracy deliberately produced by The Peoples' Representatives, known as The WIZARD

This state of war shall exist UNTIL: either The City Council shows signs of responding to popular opinion and to informed advice concerning the matters raised in The Wizard's correspondence by appointing him

ARCHWIZARD OF CANTERBURY

OR

The Wizard, who is rapidly becoming a major tourist attraction in addition to his functions as raiser of community morale, provoker of ideas and defuser of fanatics,

IS

finally forced to submit to the ignorant ill-mannered enmity of the Christchurch City Councillors

BY

giving up his last ditch stand in Cathedral Square and abandoning the city to the ravages of The Peoples' Representatives who are ignorantly destroying the very people who elected them.

Ian B Channell

Cosmologer by Appointment to Melbourne University Union
Wizard by Appointment to the World University Service
(Australia) & Canterbury Council of Calligraphers
Prophet by Appointment to Christchurch Technical Institute
Students' Association
Founder and Leader of the Imperial British Conservative Party
Generalissimo of Alf's Imperial Army
Chairman of the Home Rule for The West Coast movement.

Demonic possession

There were many born-agains in the Square out to save sinners. I managed to get most fundamentalists to admit that they believed the Pope was the Antichrist, which put off many potential converts. I denied this strongly since I had already claimed the title of Antichrist for myself at Melbourne. The legend of the Antichrist describes him as a brilliant orator who holds crowds enthralled and whose aim is to ascend to heaven without the help of God and without dying. As he starts to ascend, God sends his archangels to strike him down. This dramatic event having taken place, Christ comes again. Who else in the world fitted this description better than myself?

I also claimed that I was born again myself. Everything about me indicated that I had been through some sort of transforming experience. I also pointed out that my lifestyle was now astonishingly similar to that of Jesus: I had no job, no wife, no children, no property, no welfare from the state and spent my life addressing crowds with the good news that I had arrived.

I had been 'sent' a white plastic telephone receiver which I called my 'Hotline to Heaven'. When confidently informed that I was going to hell, I would pick up the hotline and check the accuracy of the statement. My information was that no one really knew whether they were going there or not: even I was not certain. We had to live in hope. The people with the best chance, however, were enclosed nuns, who practised poverty, chastity and obedience and prayed quietly all hours of the day and night.

I would always give the born-agains the benefit of my wisdom and repeated many wise sayings of Jesus. As I'm sure the reader is aware, trying to get through to a humourless religious or political fanatic is a complete waste of time, but the crowds loved it.

War declared on city fathers

Although I had become one of the city's foremost tourist attractions, I was getting nowhere with the council in my applications to give free lectures or act as their prophet, but I thought that at least they would accept me as a professional exhibitionist and free entertainer as their living work of art.

They did not even reply to my letters. Direct action was required to force them to the sub-committee room. I issued an ultimatum that, unless they answered my letter and showed some sign of at least considering my offer, a state of artistic war would exist between us. The talented and loyal Alice, who is a gifted calligrapher, designed a poster-sized ultimatum.

My splendid Declaration of War on the Christchurch City Council.

No reply was received so I declared war. Wearing a kind of Roman soldier's uniform I led my large crowd (including the Bible Lady, who would do anything for publicity) to the council chambers and delivered an even more beautiful Declaration of War. The newspapers had a field day. Shortly afterwards the relevant sub-committee met, while I made an exhibition of myself outside on the pavement. They just made oafish jokes, and voted against my offer.

By the end of 1975 I had still received no reply to my request to be appointed city wizard. They had not even considered the proposal. The tourist potential was the most obvious advantage. In all the guide books about New Zealand my appearances in the Square were being described as a must for visitors and I had achieved great local popularity.

Finally, after refusing for eighteen months even to put the matter on their agenda, on 26 January 1976, the cultural committee of the council, headed by the highly opinionated Helen Garrett (who simply dismissed all theories of conceptual art as 'a load of rubbish'), actually discussed my proposal to serve the city in a voluntary capacity. By a vote of five to three they rejected the proposal. Since I was obviously a frivolous individual who did things for fun, the council would only damage its reputation by associating itself with me. Even debating the issue was a waste of their precious time.

Things did not look good for my future in Christchurch. I had overestimated the intelligence and sense of humour of the council. I began to cast my eyes on other possible bases for my wizardry. A few weeks later, mayors from Auckland, Wellington and Dunedin, in town for a conference, were quizzed by Bruce Ansley, the foremost columnist in the *Star*, about how they felt about the possibility of my shifting to their cities. Impressed with how much I had done to bring character and colour to Christchurch, they all said they would welcome my presence.

Launching the Imperial British Conservative Party

A few months earlier I had completed my preparations for the creation of a new political party and fielded a couple of candidates in the general election at the end of 1975. I had tried out the idea of such a party a few years earlier and had stood three times in the Australian federal elections before I was ready to sit down and write *The Foundations of the Imperial British Conservative Party*, a document setting out the historical background, the ground rules and the broad policies of the party.

The IBC Party was, and still is, unique in a number of ways, apart from the fact that the initials are a kind of memorial to Ian Brackenbury Channell, who had died that the Wizard might live. We were also the first party this century in the Western world who aimed to drastically reduce and finally abolish compulsory taxation and compulsory secular education and to hand back the running of welfare institutions to charitable trusts and religious organisations. This was in the early 1970s, almost fifteen years before this idea was even hinted at in political circles.

Other radically different policies included the revival and expansion of the honours system to motivate good behaviour, combined with the removal of the power of party politicians to grant honours and the return of this practice to the monarchy acting under advice. We also recommended the re-establishment of upper houses of parliament, where political parties were banned and whose members were appointed by the monarch.

Another policy that produced laughter or shocked horror was our proposal for the re-establishment of the Anglican church in Canada, Australia and New Zealand. This would be accompanied by the disestablishment of economic determinism as the official belief system. I could at last use the word 'antidisestablishmentarianism'!

A Wizard choice — Alice as a parliamentary candidate in 1975.

I carry on regardless

I tried without success to interest influential people in my party. I could get no comments at all from any political scientists, theologians or journalists who were not prepared to comment on it, let alone enter into dialogue. But I persuaded Alice and a friend of mine, Brian Downham, to stand for parliament as IBC candidates that November, and the mother of another friend of mine, with strong views on education, stood at a by-election in Nelson early in 1976.

In those days there were really only three political parties in New Zealand and a handful of independents. My candidates, regarded as freaks, didn't get enough votes to recover their deposits and had to pay their own election expenses. At least we attracted attention and if people shared our distrust of the almost identical policies of the main parties they knew that at least someone was standing up to be counted with a developed political philosophy and not just a malcontent or single-issue fanatic.

Alf's Imperial Army

These early years were the time when my non-violent Alf's Imperial Army really took off in New Zealand. Colonel Tony Catford had been sent from Melbourne to Christchurch a year ahead of me to prepare the way and did a fine job setting up regiments in the main centres. Most of the recruits came from the universities and battles were usually fought on the campuses.

Canterbury University, with its landscaped terrain and wide stream in front of the student union building, was an ideal battleground. Sometimes hundreds of students would turn out to oppose Alf's Imperial Army, who, with their pith helmets, red jackets and banners, would march on to the campus with drums and bugles to crush anti-imperialism and republicanism with rolled newspaper swords and flour bombs. Battles soon began at Massey, Otago and Victoria Universities and sometimes, to our surprise, at the trendy radical Auckland campus.

An amazing TV appearance

My brief period as a talkback host on Radio Avon, which many people remember with delight, was a great help in combating the impression given by journalists that, although I was an amusing figure, my ideas were basically stupid or quite mad. I was also fortunate that, at the end of 1975, skilled interviewer Brian Edwards invited me on to his TV programme *Edwards on*

Slaughter at Ilam — Alf's Imperial Army in battle at the university.

Saturday and gave me my head. Then he had the invited studio audience heckle me while I gave a demonstration of a performance in Cathedral Square. The rather ignorant listeners simply shouted over me without listening to a word. It made good television, however, and the reviews were ecstatic.

That was the last time I was given an opportunity in the mass media to make even the simplest explanation of the ideas involved in my failed attempt to attempt to levitate from the Antipodes Islands. I am constantly amazed at people's lack of curiosity and ignorance of metaphysics. I have printed and distributed at least 100,000 copies of my upside-down New World Map which indicates my own mean time ('now' is still 4 December 1974, until further notice) and my own mean place ('here', which is still the Antipodes Islands).

I realised that the 'objective' and 'subjective' centres of the universe are still separate. That's why my thought experiment involves uniting both temporarily by becoming the centre of world attention, 'me'. Then at this specific moment in time ('now') I would attempt to ascend from my subjective centre (the Antipodes Islands) into the objective centre of the universe. I still regard this as the most beautiful, benevolent and logical thought experiment ever designed. A perfect example of an existential 'leap of faith'.

An obscene martyr?

About this time I appeared in court charged with using obscene language and was found guilty!

For over a year my sneaky fundamentalist enemies had been concealing themselves in my crowds, waiting for me to make a mistake so they could pounce. The occasion came when I was trying to explain the Oedipus complex to a particularly thick and insensitive heckler. The police were called and arrived immediately and I was charged with using obscene language.

This was really unfair since all around me in the Square I had been hearing the same word being shouted out with monotonous regularity by the louts who frequent public places. At university the air was thick with obscene language from both staff and students, and the word I used was then commonly heard in films. Ironically I have been regarded by many as a prude because I never use obscene language and on this occasion I broke my rule only because it was a wonderful chance for a great dramatic moment.

To my amazement the magistrate found me guilty, saying that a man in my position should set an example. What position? I was financially down and out, a street entertainer regarded by many as a madman, was not in a position of trust over young people, and the council did not want a bar of me. As it was a 'misdemeanour', I did not appeal the judgment and was fined $30 and costs. My regular audience, furious at the magistrate's finding, wrote letters to the newspapers on my behalf and, without any prompting from me, took up a collection and paid the fine and costs on my behalf. I've been told that no one in New Zealand had been charged and found guilty of obscene language (without any other charges) for decades. I believe mine was also the last case.

I mention this case to show how my enemies were always waiting for me to commit a tiny error. Primitive shamans are described as having to walk along a razor's edge. It comes with the territory and explains why there are so few wizards and so many foul-mouthed and truly obscene pseudo-feminist witches supported by the taxpayer in tertiary teaching positions. Who would dare to take one of them to court?

11

Putting the fear of God into the census authorities

My status as a postmodern, postindividualist with no 'rights' was threatened when the five-yearly census was held early in 1976. If I completed the form as required I would be forced back into my old modern, individualistic and legal identity as Ian Channell.

I could easily have dodged the census as I was not even in Christchurch at the time and received no form, but my honour was at stake. Dressed in my best black gown and pointy hat, I took the Prophet's Declaration of Independence from the Secular Inquisition to the office of the Government Statistician, Ernie Harris. He would not even come out of his office to receive it and I had to leave it with his secretary. Over the years my battles concerning the census led to my becoming quite friendly with Mr Harris's successor, who told me that the former was genuinely scared by my dramatic appearance in his inner sanctum.

Putting the fear of God into Ernie Harris. Four years later, The Press reported an astonishing piece of news that had hitherto been suppressed: no sooner had I left the building than there was a power failure and every light went out!

EVENING POST

95

Prosecuted at last

Finally I was prosecuted and fortunately, Doug Taffs, who had just begun to practise law, agreed to handle the case for me. Knowing that I lived in very poor circumstances he would accept my own currency (Heavenly Credits), which I had recently produced, as sufficient reward.

Of course the courts and the newspapers weren't interested in such irrelevant topics as the use of force to ensure compliance with unproductive questionnaires, or religious concerns with the growth of the power of the secular government. Even my point that random sampling would produce more accurate results than a census was never commented on. My status as a living work of art was imperilled, but there was no interest in this either. Trivial points of law are what really count in a blind, ritualistic civilisation and the basis of our defence was the expiry of the statutory period before prosecution.

Continuously offensive

The Magistrates Court did not agree that this was the case. The Crown successfully argued that my not filling my census form was a 'continuing offence'. Since the census is, by its very nature, an event restricted in time to a twelve-hour period, to claim that someone can still be failing to fill in his form over a year later was absurd nonsense. They were desperate to teach me lesson in humility. They also doubled the statutory fine.

The continuing continuing offence

On my behalf, Doug Taffs lodged an appeal to the Supreme Court. A year later, in May 1978, we were in court again. This time I wore a purple robe in deference to the status of the court.

Mr Justice Roper, although agreeing that the Crown's notion of the continuing offence was absurd, considered that the previous fine was excessive and halved it, but still insisted that I pay court costs and legal fees. The harsh fine was unnecessary because this was 'hardly the type of charge which required a deterrent sentence to stop others of like mind because there were not many others of like mind'.

Off to sea for the Noncensus Party in 1981.

Fat last!

It need hardly be said that we appealed once again, this time to the Court of Appeal, where the charge was dismissed and I was awarded all costs. I burned a census form in Cathedral Square to celebrate my victory. The government was forced to amend the Census Act to make it prophet-proof, but they neglected to make it wizard-proof.

All at sea over the census

Partly inspired by my beloved *Hunting of the Snark,* and partly by childhood reading of pirate tales, when the census of 1981 approached I decided to find another loophole through which to make my escape.

I decided to hold a Noncensus Party at sea, was just outside New Zealand's twelve-mile zone of political control. I had found a yachtsman of strong character who was not easily intimidated by anyone, the legendary Albion

THE PRESS

Wright of Pegasus Press fame, who agreed to take me out the necessary distance in his famous boat, *Pastime*, which had carried the ashes of that wonderful character and talented poet Denis Glover to his final resting place. Dick Taylor, a round-the-world yachtsman, agreed to organise a fleet of boats to accompany us to the Noncensus Party.

Cowardly yachties

Alas, on the day the other yachtsmen turned out to be cowardly blowhards who found all sorts of excuses why they couldn't make the trip! Dick Taylor accompanied our single boat by windsurfing all around us. I was joined on the boat by two other wizards, Wayne, from Dunedin, and Tony, from Wellington and by the anti-wizard, Murgatroyd, of no fixed address. With us was John Blumsky, who broadcast regular reports of our position on National Radio when he was not being violently seasick.

At midnight, surrounded by the blazing lights of Japanese squid boats, we took bearings to establish that we were more than twelve miles off the coast and I let off some fireworks, blew my bugle and celebrated our triumph over the evil census.

Calling the government's bluff

Everyone, including the Statistics Department, seemed to think that, because New Zealand had a 200-mile exclusive economic zone for fishing rights and so on, I would still be in territorial waters and would have to fill in my census form or face prosecution. In a radio interview with me, census officials stated emphatically that, by going out to sea, I wasn't avoiding my legal obligation to fill in the questionnaire.

When we returned we found two shivering bureaucrats on the dock waiting for us. They thrust census forms into our hands and departed, their job done. But they didn't stand a chance in court. After all, we were surrounded by Japanese squid boats and their crews who weren't obliged to fill in census forms. The irony was that everyone knew exactly who and where we were but they couldn't put it down on a government form.

I did not hear another word from Ernie Harris and his henchmen. A year later, as I had in 1976, I repeated the ceremony of the burning of the census form in Cathedral Square in front of an appreciative audience.

12
My good works

'Wizard Save the Queen'

The first time young British Imperialists and their wizard mentors attracted the attention of the British monarchy was in 1977 when Queen Elizabeth and Prince Philip were met by imperialists at various points in their tour of the South Island and by a wizard in Christchurch. The Queen was amused and Prince Philip was intrigued.

Realising that New Zealand politicians and bureaucrats were fast becoming victims of Americanisation and were daily turning more republican, we expected them to make and less fuss over Royal Visits. We had paper Union

While visiting Dunedin in 1981 Prince Charles chats with a trio of wizards as members of Alf's Imperial Army stand to attention alongside.

OTAGO DAILY TIMES

Jacks printed, stuck them on sticks, and sold them to the crowds just before the Royals arrived. A forest of waving Union Jacks awaited them wherever there were wizards and imperialists at work behind the scenes; otherwise there was nothing. I also produced 'Wizard Save the Queen' buttons.

Since the Royals were always accompanied by a mob of pressmen we staged elaborate set pieces in honour of the Queen. One of these was a *tableau vivant* of 'Imperialism Victorious', where magnificent red-jacketed men with their shining gold buttons and freshly blancoed pith helmets posed, holding a Union Jack aloft in a very stylish manner.

On another occasion (having first got the go-ahead from the police in charge of security at Christchurch airport) we mounted one of our large plastic-barrelled cannons on a grassy knoll at the roundabout where the airport road debouches on to the main road into town. It was, of course, pointed away from the road. The sight of five wizards silhouetted against the sky behind a large cannon unnerved the driver of the Royal car, who unfortunately had not been informed of this official wizards' welcome, and he put on an extra turn of speed so that Her Majesty did not have time to fully appreciate the fine sight of the wizards firing their well-known weapon (usually filled with lollies).

I print my own money

The Heavenly Credits, which I had used to reward my lawyer and kind people who gave me lifts when I was hitch-hiking, etc., had also been my way of beating the inflation that was being produced when the Muldoon government began printing too much money. In 1977 I printed a few thousand Heavenly Credits, each individually numbered and personally signed by me as 'Chief Cashier of the Bank of Heaven'. Each note bore a picture of me looking inspired and of HM Queen Elizabeth, as Defender of the Faith, looking radiantly happy.

I took the notes to the Square and, having explained the difference between honour and greed and between earthly treasure and heavenly treasure, I sold my Heavenly Credits for $1 each. Then I set fire to the dollar bills, often quite a large number, as a worthy sacrifice to God. For those who

My fight against inflation. Using a small metal replica of the Statue of Liberty as a holder, and after blowing my bugle and crying out in a loud voice, I set fire to dollar bills, often quite a large number, as a worthy sacrifice to God. Once the bills had been reduced to ashes, I checked on my hotline to see if my sacrifice had been received in heaven. When I nodded my head in pleasure at the answer the crowd cheered with gusto.

complained I had another answer: by burning the banknotes that the government was printing so profusely, I was reducing the number of notes in circulation and was thereby a hero in the fight against inflation.

Prophet versus priest

In 1978 I finally enticed two of my favourite Anglican clergymen, Bob Lowe and Dean Michael Underhill, to come out of their cosy but rather empty churches into the hustle and bustle of the world. Arriving in the Square one day, I found the dean was doing his best on a soapbox outside the cathedral. I can do no better than quote *The Press* on its front page: 'The Dean had been . . . talking to what he described as "a rather small crowd", when the Wizard arrived with his much larger throng of lunch-time supporters. "I had just got started when he came," said Dean Underhill. "I was a little frightened that it might have been the end of our little talk, but I must admit that the Wizard was on his best behaviour. He certainly boosted the crowd and he gave me 50 percent of the time."'

On reflection, Dean Underhill thought there had been 'a grain of truth' in most things the Wizard had said. 'He says that every religion has to have a priest and a prophet. When the priest gets a bit old and heavy, the prophet comes along with new ideas.'

I face a loose canon

A couple of weeks later Canon Bob Lowe, vicar of Fendalton parish, came to do battle. He was a formidable opponent. Not only had he, like me, stood at the feet of the great speakers at Tower Hill in London, but he had extensive media experience as a regular broadcaster of colourful cricket commentaries, delivered powerful sermons each Sunday, and had a huge chest and a voice to match. Moreover he had a microphone and loudhailer and his back up against the cathedral walls.

I must confess that he was a match for me. The Anglican church looked as though it was fighting back, but it was the last time. Towards the end of our well-attended dialogue an army of about a thousand women appeared waving banners and chanting androphobic war-cries through loudspeakers. It was the apogee of the worldwide feminist movement and the first big celebration of International Women's Day.

Dean Mike Underhill and I make the front page of The Press.

Women of the world unite against men

As the last heroic defender of free speech in New Zealand, I held my ground in my customary corner of the Square, although my heart beat faster. From the corner of my eye I saw a young man who dared pass a remark about the women being grabbed, turned upside down and dumped into a rubbish bin.

The women formed a huge circle and began to dance like a coven of witches claiming territory. Since they were armed with amplification devices and had the rest of the Square to themselves, I carried on speaking, unamplified, to my well-disciplined crowd.

To my surprise, policemen appeared, showed me a note from the council announcing the closure of Speakers' Corner and told me I must cease. Knowing that the council did not control cathedral territory, I moved my ladder further into the cathedral precinct and continued my speech.

Once again I was approached by the police, who said that if I continued I would be arrested for breaching the peace since my presence might inflame the mob of feminists into an act of violence against me. This was a tricky situation. I consulted my Hotline to Heaven. Being arrested for such a stupid reason was not heaven's will, so I left my ladder and mingled with the crowd to watch the extraordinary spectacle of mass hysteria. It was essentially council-funded and police-protected sexism!

I am not opposed to women's rights to be like men, however foolish the ambition. To the contrary, as my listeners will testify, I have always actively encouraged the idea in my speeches. I like women to be as honest, passionate and stupid as men. It's those who think they are magical sex-objects or moral mother-goddesses who incur my criticism.

13
Feminism and a postnuclear family structure

My experiments in producing a postmodern family structure in Melbourne had not been successful, but Alice had stuck with me and was proving her worth in every way. She had become an intellectual colleague, loyal friend and mutual sharer of aesthetic experiences; she even watched television with me. She had also broadened my horizons by introducing me to a wide range of religious professionals and their interests. My aim had always been to build an enduring relationship between male and female which was not based on fertility or economic benefits and which would be more stable than the present system of serial monogamy.

Alice watches me watching TV.

In 1977, within a few months of each other, two young women were showing signs that they might be suitable as 'slaves', although they would have to accept Alice's seniority. I did not for one moment think that Alice would approve of this, since she is a one-man woman with strong religious views.

In my own defence, my relationship with Alice began on the assumption that she would have to share me with two or three others. I had no wish to project my masculine polygamous nature on to women who seemed to be strongly monogamous (at least 'one at a time'). Nor do I accept women projecting their deeply monogamous nature on to me and judging me as immoral if I don't live up to their expectations.

I have never been promiscuous; to me sexuality has inevitable psychological aspects so powerful that I feel responsible for the mental and spiritual wellbeing of my partners and could not possibly use them simply as means to my emotional ends. Consequently I cannot stand being looked after by a women in an emotional sense: I don't expect security or sexual pleasure from them.

I act on the assumption that the male-female relationship is essentially reciprocal at the biological, psychological and, to some extent, the social level, but at the spiritual or cultural level it is foolish to try and make distinctions.

I knew it would hurt Alice to bring other women into my life, and therefore hers, but I had earlier put in writing the set of rights and obligations that comprised my new marriage system. I've gone to enormous lengths and overcome some formidable obstacles in order to gain ownership of my own body. I do not surrender it easily to another's possession.

After a few months I allowed the other two young women to become involved, after making sure they understood the rules that bound my behaviour towards them. If they had any doubts, they should find a man who was more amenable to female 'behaviour modification'.

Irresistible force meets immovable object

Alice was sick with jealousy. I was not so insensitive as to expect her to meet the others or hear about them from me. My reassurances that she was number one 'wife', as in the numerous cultures that allow polygamy, made no difference. Nor did my arguments that compulsory monogamy was a radical new development in marriage systems, developed by the Romans and carried over into Christianity and recently forced on to the rest of the world through European imperialism. She was not responding with her intellect.

This was a tragic situation, a real impasse. I owed so much to Alice's loyal support in times of crisis; she was truly part of me. Both of us are extremely outspoken, principled and stubborn individuals. Her pain was largely emotional, mine was largely intellectual; I could empathise with her suffering, but I couldn't betray myself to stop it.

I lose Alice . . . but only physically

The emotional storms having failed to make me knuckle under, Alice, feeling unloved and in a strange land, returned to her family in Melbourne at the end of 1977. Having found a responsible post in the Tracing Agency of the Australian Red Cross, she went back to university part time to study for another honours degree, this time in fine arts.

Alice was not prepared to abandon her commitment to me and get involved with some unsuitably weak-minded man on the rebound. She rang me every week and we corresponded regularly. As far as she was concerned, she would wait and see what happened.

My last attempt to control women

For a few months all went well. The older girl, whom I began to call Tinkerbell on account of her love of dancing and superficially lively and confident behaviour, took a sisterly interest in the welfare of the younger, who was escaping from her difficult family circumstances. Tinkerbell, too, had a troubled background. She stood for parliament a couple of times, the first time for the seat of Lyttelton, where she stood against

Tinkerbell and the Wizard, 1978.

DOMINION & SUNDAY TIMES

four women and a single man with the slogan 'Put a Fairy into Parliament'.

Tinkerbell stood again for a by-election in Christchurch Central the following year. Her slogan was 'Slavery for Women'. This was to contrast with other candidates whose policies were to use political, legal and economic pressure to make men softer and more servile. On another occasion, at a Wanganui rock festival, I took her around with me on a lead and harness with bells attached. In Christchurch I used to hitch her lead round a verandah post outside a pub while I went inside for a drink. If anyone came up to feel sorry for her she would promptly put them in their place.

At first Tinkerbell was glad to have a stable relationship, but that attitude changed and in 1981 she left on an overseas trip. Meanwhile, although we were certainly a union of opposites, I was finding my relationship with the other young woman challenging if somewhat nerve-racking.

The Wizard returns in triumph to Oz

In 1980, David Chapman of the Government Tourist Bureau in Melbourne, a very innovative public servant, decided that, since I was such a popular attraction for tourists coming to New Zealand, I should be brought to Victoria for a major promotion involving appearances on radio programmes and giving newspaper interviews.

This was a breakthrough for me and succeeded beyond David Chapman's wildest dreams. I received wonderful publicity in Australia and when I returned to New Zealand the papers there praised me as a great ambassador for the country.

Together again

When I was in Australia Alice had just returned from a trip to India with her friends from her ashram. (She had been interested in yoga for years and had become a swami while still attending mass every Sunday and singing in her church choir.) She made it clear that although she was still 'in my spell', she couldn't bear to be in the same town as any other woman I had anything to do with. This was fair enough, I thought, and we agreed that later she should come over to New Zealand for a holiday. (This proved to be like a honeymoon; we had never before spent so much time together and we got on like a house on fire.)

This photo was taken to mark my appointment as Archwizard of Canterbury.

Archwizard of Canterbury

Bruce Dunstan, the newly appointed public relations officer for Canterbury, not just for Christchurch, had been very impressed not only with the spectacular success of the Australian promotion but also with my role in bringing tourists to the region.

Bruce contacted all the local-government authorities who made up the Canterbury Promotion Council, of which he was the executive officer, and in May 1980 persuaded them that they should officially appoint me Archwizard of Canterbury and advertise my presence in the Square in their excellent visitors' guide.

CHRIS PALMER

14

Travails of a living work of art

My last chance to fall through the earth

I had hypothesised that I had only seven years before my nervous system became too old to enable me to harness the universal levitational force, rise in the air, vanish and accelerate faster than light as a pure thought. Passing through the centre of the universe, I would descend on the other side of the hollow earth. Murgatroyd the anti-wizard had gone on ahead to London to prepare the way.

His arrival had caused something of a stir. Immigration officials were reluctant to admit a rather oddly dressed individual whose stated purpose of visit was to prepare for the arrival of the Archwizard of Canterbury, who would fall from the sky at Tower Hill in London, site of my early inspiration.

Murgatroyd had constructed a twelve-foot-high bamboo tower with rubber strips as a catching device. While in London making these preparations, he did radio broadcasts and gave interviews to the press. The sheer originality of the idea was stunning and exceeded the wildest dreams of science fiction and fantasy writers. I believe the story has now entered the collective unconscious of the English people.

Final failure

Once again I could get no support whatsoever to get a boat to the Antipodes Islands in time for my thought experiment. I pointed out to various media organisations that it would make a wonderful story, especially on TV. Their warped emotions and limited intelligences didn't enable them to grasp the fact that, whether it worked or not, they had an absolute winner in terms of ratings. I was already famous for my boat trip to avoid the census.

That was my last chance to beat death and gravity by transcending the world physically and metaphysically. I am not a dualist who believes that the soul is something quite separate from the body and can make the trip to heaven or be reincarnated after the death of the body.

I had become friends with Wendy and John De La Bere, who were passionately involved in the religious and theatrical life of Christchurch. Wendy decided to stage the medieval Everyman morality play in the cathedral. Impressed with my histrionic skills, she persuaded me to play the part of God the Father.

There was a bit of a furore and the dean caught a lot of flak. I thought I made a good job of it. Christchurch, like other places, is full of people playing God and I looked the part

better than most. The Press photographer, who put a picture of me of me in my costume on the front page, 'enhanced' the photo with a suggestion of a halo.

Also in the firing line at this time was the telephone company, who had put a child's painting of the Square (featuring me) on the cover of the new phone book. One enthusiastic fundamentalist wrote to the paper expressing their horror and saying that they had cut a hole in the cover to remove my image from their home.

Magic staff

During the full eclipse of the eclipse of the moon in 1982 I was presented with a beautifully twisted and elaborately carved staff of power. This had been carved by Michael Smith from Southland, who spent a year finding the right piece of wood and carving it into the right shape. He presented me with staff as a free offering and was content to receive a scroll from me acknowledging him as 'Wood Carver by Appointment to the Wizard'.

Blessings

I was kept pretty busy performing blessings at all sorts of occasions – new businesses, school and church fairs, conferences, festivals of all kinds. The mayor would do openings and I would perform the ritual blessings. This is still my main public function now that most priests have become secularised and have stopped wearing their robes to become rather like social workers. Meanwhile journalists from overseas newspapers and magazines were writing glowing reports on my stimulating presence in New Zealand and I was travelling all over the country to perform and carry out blessings.

Travel thwarted

I received an invitation to appear in the 1984 Adelaide Arts Festival Fringe but, owing to a burst of chauvinism by the Labor government of Australia, who decided in 1981 that New Zealanders were to lose their special relationship and must have passports like any other foreigners, I was faced with the problem of getting a passport and becoming a 'real person' again without losing the special identity I had so painstakingly built up.

I decided to make a real effort to get there as a living work of art. I found the Immigration Minister, Aussie Malcolm, most appreciative of my dilemma and he began communicating with the various ministers and public servants across the Tasman to find a way to get me to Australia, not as a legal person but as a work of art. The correspondence makes wonderful reading and Aussie told me it was one of most enjoyable things he did in office.

Crating a precedent

While the arguments were raging, I provided a precedent by arranging to have myself transported from the Christchurch City Art Gallery to the Auckland City Art Gallery in a crate. This was possible because Rodney Wilson, the lively young director of the Christchurch gallery, who had transferred

AUCKLAND CITY ART GALLERY
Receipt for deposited works

OWNER _NATIONAL GALLERY of_   ARTIST _IAN BRACKENBURY CHANNELL_

ADDRESS _VICTORIA_   TITLE _The wizard of Christchurch_

MELBOURNE   MEDIUM _artist's corporeal substance_

PHONE pvte._____ bus._____   VALUE _priceless_   ~~FRAMED~~/UNFRAMED

CONSIDER FOR PURCHASE ☐   LOAN FOR EXHIBITION ☐

APPRAISAL BY CURATOR ☑   APPRAISAL BY CONSERVATOR ☑

LOAN TO PERMANENT COLLECTION from_____ to_____

SIGNED_____ DATE _2 : III : 1984_
ON BEHALF OF THE AUCKLAND CITY ART GALLERY

NOTE: Works brought into the Gallery, are NOT covered by insurance, and are entirely at owner's risk.

On consignment.

my title as living work of art from Melbourne, was now director of the Auckland gallery.

At the beginning of March I was dispatched in the same manner as any other work of art. All the proper forms were filled in and I was crated up (with some liquid refreshment). With the cameras whirring, I waved farewell and played a muffled fanfare on my bugle as the crate was picked up to be transported to the airport. I was unpacked and checked for damage at the Auckland gallery and went on to make an exhibition of myself, though of course I had already done that.

What a brilliant synthesis of conceptual art, re-enchanting the world, and political action for love and freedom. Our local conceptual artist Billy Apple has become famous on the basis of much less imaginative ideas.

I was crated up again and dispatched to the Hawke's Bay Art Gallery a few months later. During my appearance there, a local art critic and the living work of art got into an argument and ended up wresting on the floor among the public. I found this personally very satisfying.

Art fights back

Meanwhile the cables and phone calls between the New Zealand and the Australian immigration departments were mounting up without a satisfactory outcome. Whatever the New Zealand authorities proposed by interpreting various clauses in government legislation relating to works of art, valuable national treasures, or even livestock was rejected by the minister in Australia. Even the intervention of the our High Commissioner in Canberra could not alter the rigid line of the Australians.

Sports & Leisure

YOUR CONVENIENT
SPORTS CLOTHING
AND EQUIPMENT STORE

Open till 8.30pm Thursdays
9am — 12 Noon Saturday
Phone 68 339

The Hawke's Bay
Herald-Tribun

Thursday, August 23, 1984. Telephone 85 155 All Departments Price 30c. HOME DE

A living work of art arrived in Napier yesterday.

The Wizard of Christchurch was unpacked at Hawke's Bay Airport, after arriving as Air New Zealand freight, by Napier public relations officer Brian Cotter (left) and Civic Court retailers' representatives Graham Duncan (partly obscured) and Dean Dickey (right).

The Wizard's consignment slip and artistic licence were checked by Hawke's Bay Art Gallery and Museum staff Roslyn Hoek and Anna Bibby, who took delivery of the "exhibit."

The Wizard is in town until Sunday and was to be casting spells and reciting incantations at the official opening of the new Civic Court shopping centre this afternoon.

Tonight he will be speaking at the Hawke's Bay Art Gallery and Museum on his status as a living work of art, and will be leading an informal debate on related topics.

The Wizard, with clowns Raspberry and Lumpy Custard, will be making merry at the Civic Court again tomorrow morning.

The Wizard, created by Ian Brackenbury-Channel, was designated a work of art in 1972 and is presently on loan to the Robert McDougall Gallery in Christchurch.

"This means that instead of standing around being a pretty little poofter, I get out and produce bizarre effects in the community," he says of his designation.

He's happy about the fact that he's "no longer officially a human being" because he hasn't got the right papers, but instead has documents proving his status as an art work.

In August 1984, I arrive in Napier as a living work of art.

Alice gets a medal and cognitive therapy

In 1983 Alice, together with other Red Cross members, had gone to a psychologist for counselling as a result of the stress they'd suffered during the terrible Ash Wednesday fires in Victoria. Alice had been awarded the Red Cross Meritorious Service Medal for her work but was emotionally and physically exhausted. I thoroughly approved of the psychologist, Diana Elton, whose no-nonsense rational cognitive approach was a great help to Alice. Hearing about me, she was fascinated but also told Alice that, in her place, she would have killed me!

One slave departs and another returns

Meanwhile my experimental relationship with my remaining 'slave' in Christchurch was going badly wrong. The trouble started when she wanted to have a child and she knew that I was resolutely against being turned into a father. By 1985 she had had a child by another man and had decided that it was all over between us. I was greatly relieved, but not half so much as Alice.

In 1984 Tinkerbell had made a hair-raising escape from Morocco, where her life had been a nightmare, leaving a Muslim husband and child behind her. She wanted to cool off and calm down and was keen to put what money into a house that she would share with me, Alice, and my old colleague from Melbourne University, David Sutton. On the assurance that my intimacy with Tinkerbell was at an end, and knowing that 'number three' had permanently left the scene, Alice also put some money into the house and came over to live with us for an experimental six months. I was going to live in proper house again after seventeen years of living in cheap rooms! But I was also living in the same house as a woman again. Was I going soft?

It was a difficult time and Alice was much happier when, after couple of years, we sold up and bought a much larger house. David got a place of his own. My mother, independent to the last, finally admitting she could no longer cope on her own, sold up and took a share in the new place.

I keep my mother in a wardrobe

In 1987 Alice made the move back from Australia and, together with my mother, Tinkerbell and me, took up residence in the old Victorian homestead. It was already partly divided into flats so it was easy for everyone to have their own completely independent quarters and my mother could have a well-appointed 'granny flat'. I arranged access to this through the back of a large cupboard in our hallway. This tickled her fancy and intrigued our friends, who made remarks about the Witch in the Wardrobe.

Alice finally gets her man

My mother died in 1990 and, soon after, Tinkerbell left to become a Feldenkreis instructor. Finally I was living with Alice, who had nailed me at last but also found herself owning a large house and similarly large mortgage. She got a loan from her ever-supportive parents and she let three flats, which would pay the interest and a little more. We lived in the rest of the house, which was big enough for me to have my set of rooms and stay sane.

With Alice.

15

The hazards of casting spells for rugby matches

A word of warning

Since I have achieved a certain amount of notoriety for my attempts to influence the outcome of important rugby matches in New Zealand I feel I should set the record straight. Life is not always easy for those of us in the magical profession. I must take this opportunity to warn young wizards or to those readers who have not yet chosen their careers but are considering wizardry as an option.

I began my community spell-casting with such simple thaumaturgical operations as blessing new shopping malls and business enterprises or local school and church fêtes. Following on these activities I was asked to bless the odd local sports team setting out for an 'away' match.

Then, in late August 1984, almost exactly ten years after my arrival in Christchurch, I was invited by the Auckland Rugby Football Supporters Club to travel to Auckland to attend a coaches' dinner to raise money for the Otara Spinal Unit and invited to go out on the field just before the match to cast a victory spell for Canterbury.

It was one of the most important rugby games for years. Canterbury were the proud holders of the Ranfurly Shield, or 'Log o' Wood'. I was to go on to the field just before the match in front of the crowd of 40,000, most of whom were fanatical Auckland supporters. Going out to mutter the necessary cantrips and mantras while performing extravagant gestures with a flaming flare, I found I was not alone. Three strange figures of gigantic proportions appeared and pranced alongside me. I found out later that these were the legendary cult figures Polly, Snowy and Loosehead Len. This was certainly unexpected competition.

When I went to take my seat in the VIP box, in the row behind me was the Prime Minister, the Leader of the Opposition and, if my memory serves me right, the Primate of the Anglican Church in New Zealand.

Doomed!

I cannot bring myself to give a blow-by-blow account of that doom-stricken game. Suffice to say that Canterbury, who had not lost a single game for three years, were beaten 32–3. As we left Eden Park both the Prime Minister and the Leader of the Opposition said some very hurtful things to me and hordes of odious Auckland fans gloated loudly over my failure and Canterbury's consequent thrashing.

Resigned to my fate

I returned next day with my tail between my legs. How could I face the locals in Cathedral Square on Monday? I decided I had no choice but to bite the bullet and resign.

On Monday, 2 September, having informed the media of my intention, I

went to the Canterbury Promotion Council. Ripping off my black robes and impressive pointy hat, and dressed only in an old sack, I handed my resignation to Bruce Dunstan. National television crews recorded the sorry spectacle of me rubbing ashes into my face, tearing my long hair and beard, beating my breast and banging my head on the ground while crying out, 'Mea culpa, mea culpa, mea maxima culpa!'

Bruce tried his best to dissuade me but I was adamant. I simply could not show my face in Christchurch. Still wearing sackcloth and ashes, I proceeded to my usual speaking spot in Cathedral Square where I made a full public confession. I then announced that I was going into exile.

Mea culpa, mea culpa, mea maxima culpa!

THE PRESS

City fathers plead for me to stay

Hearing of my decision to leave Christchurch, the mayor, Sir Hamish Hay, and city councillors begged me to reconsider my decision. Schoolchildren from all over the city said it wasn't my fault and appealed to me to stay. But, in spite of this heart-warming demonstration of affection, I knew that it would be some time before I could go into any public place without being met by jeers of derision.

Following the announcement of my decision to go into exile, letters arrived at the Canterbury Promotion Council from other towns in New Zealand offering me sanctuary or just a holiday. Conjecture in Christchurch was that I might settle on their deadly rival, Auckland. Still smarting from the comments being passed about my performance at Eden Park, I informed the press that I was considering moving to the United States, whose inhabitants were badly in need of a wizard and didn't play rugby.

Whangarei welcomes Wizard

Meanwhile I received an invitation from Joyce Ryan, mayor of Whangarei, for an official visit, with a view to taking up wizardly duties there. My arrival was dramatic and well received. Accompanied by my colleague the Duke of Wellington, I was rowed into the town basin to be met by the mayor. Warm friendly people surrounded us and I felt happier than I had been for some time.

The only cloud in the sky was a demonstration by three witches, complete with broomsticks, shouting, 'Wizards go home! Our spells are better!' while I was addressing the local citizenry in the town centre. There were also some letters to the local *Northern Advocate* from indignant religious fundamentalists and signatures were being collected to oppose any proposal that I be invited to become Wizard of Whangarei.

Good news from home

While I was enjoying this break from the rugby brouhaha, I heard that the Christchurch City Council, shocked at the thought of losing their wizard, were backing a Canterbury Promotions Council scheme to set up a trust fund for me, which would provide money for such essential items as travelling expenses, costumes and fireworks. This was a welcome change of attitude by the council after years of ill-concealed hostility.

The local Radio New Zealand station, 3ZB, arranged to put a caravan in

Cathedral Square on 30 September for an all-day 'Save the Wizard Campaign' of broadcast appeals for a Wizard Trust Fund. The weather was atrocious but people came from far and wide to make their contributions, which 3ZB requested be modest, as this was a 'Wizardathon' and the Wizard's psychological medicine was much cheaper to administer than the high-tech physical medicine that was normally the beneficiary of telethons.

I give in to popular pressure

After a day of seeing little children and old-age pensioners bringing in their humble contributions, it was proving increasingly difficult to maintain my hard line about resigning.

When finally the Minister for Tourism, Mike Moore, came into the caravan and, on national television, said that not just Christchurch, but New Zealand needed a wizard, I capitulated and agreed to resume my duties as Wizard of Christchurch and Archwizard of Canterbury. I published a proclamation in the local newspapers, thanking the local people for their generous support, and resumed my unpaid duties.

Relics of the true ladder

One day in the summer of 1986 one of the rougher variety of born-agains, incensed by my criticism of the termagant Bible Lady, in a fury of righteous indignation, lifted up my wooden ladder, raised it above his head and smashed it to pieces on the ground.

My beloved old ladder. My symbol of transcendence. I have sometimes seen myself as a postmodern Jacob who wrestled with God and who had the vision of a ladder to heaven. I forgave the young man but couldn't help breaking down and crying.

Hearing of my distress, and no doubt seizing the opportunity to promote their product, an aluminium ladder company came to my rescue with a special bright red ladder with a bar to hold on to. This, which I still use, is heavy to carry and creaks rather noisily when I get carried away, but it is Christian-proof. But I still miss my old ladder.

At least it went to a good home. I presented the wreckage to the Canterbury Museum, who put it in a glass case and exhibited it along with the heart-rending story. I made a virtue of a necessity and attached fragments of the old ladder to postcards of myself as 'The Prophet', signed them as authentic and sold them to tourists as 'relics of the true ladder'.

Right: Lamenting my lost ladder.

Below: My new red ladder is clearly visible as I address a typically large crowd in Cathedral Square. This photo was made into a postcard.

THE PRESS

CHRISTCHURCH
NEW ZEALAND

16
I vanish at last

I may have failed to carry out my thought experiment and vanish from the Antipodes Islands, but I did succeed in vanishing 'legally' at the time of the 1986 census. I was able to become completely invisible for the twelve hours from midnight till noon on census day. No one saw me and I couldn't even see myself!

Before casting the elaborate spell I got from the Rosicrucian Brotherhood I wrote to the Statistics Department and to the news media to explain my intention to vanish. I attached photocopies of the relevant parts of my cosmology and some other writings.

No evidence

The enumerators were unable to find any evidence that I was physically visible during the hours of the census but, in spite of that, I was prosecuted by the department. It was an interesting court case. The prosecution case was twofold: first, there was no documentary evidence to prove I had left New Zealand and second, they did not believe I had vanished. Unfortunately my lawyer, who was the officer in charge of the local regiment of Alf's Imperial Army, was not in the best state to handle the tricky case, owing to excesses the previous night. In my legal cases I am usually the brains behind the scenes while giving the impression of being a simple layman awe-struck by the brilliance of the learned counsel. This is to avoid the risk of professional jealousy influencing the magistrate.

I listened in horror as my lawyer forgot to bring up the point that, at the previous census, there was no documentary evidence of my departure from New Zealand by boat. For all the court knew, I might have done the same thing again this time without informing the media or my friends. The magistrate relied upon natural law and stated that the man in the street would not believe I had vanished, ergo I must have been hiding somewhere. I was found guilty and fined.

I was most upset that the court had not believed that I had vanished,

When I was prosecuted by the Statistics Department in 1986, my mother was there, as was Tinkerbell in her fairy costume, a professional tea lady, a couple of imperialists — and my lawyer (at right). The magistrate had great difficulty in keeping his face straight; he had obviously had less practice than I had over the years.

even though they could produce no witness to prove the contrary. It was hardly the court's business to deal with such metaphysical matters as vanishing or where souls go when the body is no longer functioning. There was no 'point of law' involved this time so no appeal was possible.

I go on strike

I was justifiably angry that the legal profession did not think I was a wizard. Why should I go into the Square each weekday as the world-famous Wizard and give my time free for the community if I was not regarded as a wizard by the legal system?

I began wearing a convict's uniform complete with ball and chain and went to the Square to announce that I had decided to go on strike and would not appear there again until they stopped prosecuting me as a liar and a charlatan.

Months passed and the tourists were asking where I was. The tourist authorities explained that I was sulking because the government did not believe that I had vanished on census night. When there was a decent ground-swell of disappointment I put my cunning plan into operation. I drew up a number of petitions that said, 'We the undersigned believe that the Wizard vanished on Census Night and was not therefore in the country and should not be prosecuted for failing to fill in a questionnaire'. I also printed thousands of little stickers with a fierce-looking wizard's head surrounded by the words 'I BELIEVE the Wizard vanished on Census Night'.

The Canterbury Promotion Council and Information Office had the petitions on display and sent them out to other information offices all over the country. I also got stories and ads in most of the papers in New Zealand. I pointed out on TV and in the press that the people of New Zealand had a choice. Did they want a wizard who cost them nothing, cheered people up, enraged moral bullies in the churches and universities and brought wealthy American tourists to New Zealand, or did they want me to admit I was a phoney and go back to my previous job as a sincere academic sociologist?

Thousands sign

Thousands signed the petitions. Among the distinguished people who put their names down were Norm Jones, the extremely sceptical and outspoken MP for Invercargill; another MP and fan of mine, Ruth Richardson; and Sir Michael Fowler, the mayor of Wellington. As the completed petitions came in they were dispatched to parliament. I had friends who were 'moles' in the Statistics Department and they made sure my stickers appeared all over the offices there.

A subsidiary of one of the biggest firms in New Zealand paid the outstanding fine on my behalf and since I heard no more from the Statistics Department I returned triumphant to the Square to carry out the quintennial ritual of burning the Wizard's census questionnaire.

Could an ordinary man without money or power torture a large government department who had the power of the state behind them, huge sums of money and hundreds of graduates and quite a few PhDs on their payroll? It was bloody obvious I was a wizard!

Has there ever been anyone like me before? Alice thinks not, which is why she is still crazy about me after twenty-seven years. Maybe my ideas are right after all and everyone else is wrong. No wonder I have so many enemies in high places. They would lose everything if this became general knowledge.

At the end of 1987, when Leeza Gibbons of 'Entertainment This Week' came to take a good look at New Zealand, she was enchanted by the country, but especially by me. She agreed to be filmed being thrown out of the Square by my imperial forces for interrupting me during my anti-American, anti-woman and anti-Hollywood speech. When the scene went to air, viewers all over the United States went mad with delight.

Powers regained

Now that I had demonstrated my amazing powers to the world, I was ready to resume my magical support for our local rugby team, but I have to confess that this time the spell was performed during their practice session the day before they were due to play the Australian national team.

Imagine my delight, and of course the delight of the team, when they beat the Wallabies! This was all the more astonishing because the Wallabies had beaten the All Blacks that test season (1986). I was back on form and so was the team; we deserved to win.

The 1991 census

In 1991 the media were desperate to know what I was going to do about the approaching census. I felt I had caused enough trouble to the Statistics Department, who would turn pale at the mere mention of my name. The new Government Statistician, Steve Kusmevich, was polite and co-operative and even took me out to lunch. I did not want to become a bully so I decided to give them all a rest.

That year neither the statistician nor I would make any comment at all. We two are the only people who know what happened that census and we are not saying anything. Apparently this action so impressed the members of the department that, from being their worst nightmare, I became their hero.

I made life easier for everyone during the 1996 census. I now had a special Wizard's passport, so I made a trip to Australia to see my mates in Sydney.

17

The telephone box war

The Telephone Box War, which broke out in Christchurch in October 1988, was a remarkable example of a successful 'David versus Goliath' struggle. On one side, the Wizard and a few members of Alf's Imperial Army; on the other, Telecom New Zealand. The *casus belli* was the astonishing transformation of the city's wooden telephone boxes, from their traditional red to pale blue. Wherever I went I heard shocked comments about the completely pointless and disturbing nature of the change.

I don't like claiming the 'high moral ground' or giving jargon-loaded philosophical or economic reasons for what I do. I will only ever say that ultimately I do it all 'for fun'. Even more unusual, I am a radical who does not intimidate others or even break the law, though I do sometimes bend it into some rather surprising shapes. It's not often that an opportunity comes along to oppose managerial madness and malevolence without making a moral issue out of it. So a controversy over a purely aesthetic issue was an ideal opportunity for me to go on the offensive for a change.

The people feel blue and the Wizard sees red

Of Christchurch's 565 phone boxes only ninety had been painted pale blue. On Monday morning I dutifully tackled the most offensive and most prominent example of 'corporate vandalism' – the phone box beside Captain Scott's statue opposite the Christchurch Visitors' Centre. I informed the media, who recorded me carefully restoring the phone box to its original beauty, which took about two hours. In a moving ceremony I dedicated my mission to God, Queen and the Red Cross of St George. That same afternoon the henchmen of Telecom repainted it pale blue. Before nightfall I 'restored' the box again.

As this page from the Australasian Post of 21 January 1989 shows, the fame of the Telephone Box War spread far beyond the streets of Christchurch.

126

When New Zealand's Telecom decided to do some painting it started a mini-revolution which turned into a comedy . . .

The great phone box blue!

★ The Wizard Of Christchurch leads his "redvolutionary" army. ★ The Wizard stirs the public while his "redvolutionary" soldiers apply guardsman red.

From CHRIS BARCLAY

NEW Zealand's Telecom is working furiously to cover up the blue it made when it repainted Christchurch telephone boxes.

Without consultation it daubed 90 red boxes "corporate blue".

Initially it was assumed the pale blue was an undercoat. But Telecom announced that, to promote its corporate image and sever links with its predecessor, the Post Office, it had embarked on an $80,000 repainting project.

Letters to the Editor were penned. Radio talkback lines rang red-hot. And The Wizard of Christchurch — who is officially recognised as a "living work of art" — was ready to take up the cudgels against the "tasteless tyrants of Telecom" and its "poofy blue" paint jobs.

With his cronies, "Alf's Imperial Army", The Wizard set about re-painting the boxes — and the Great Telephone Box War erupted.

When members of the army re-coated the city's oldest box in Victoria Square Telecom staff watched, sharing the joke. Then, scarcely giving the box time to dry, they painted it blue again. It was all good fun until Telecom found the box red again the next morning!

Peeved, Telecom decided to bill The Wizard for $400, the cost of two coats of blue paint. But The Wizard would not be given the brush-off and declared the war would not end until each box was back to its original state.

Elsewhere in the city other would-be painters were taking brushes into their own hands. In Riccarton one turned up purple.

A Telecom survey showed 88 per cent of 10,300 people wanted red.

Telecom promised it would stand by the survey results and abandoned plans to repaint any more city boxes. However, it would not repaint existing blue boxes and any boxes vandalised would not be replaced.

This wasn't good enough for the Wizard. He announced he would paint the boxes himself and started up a "paint fund".

When his supplies dried up the city council stepped in and gave the army access to council stocks of "guardsman red".

When Telecom protested and suggested the council was encouraging acts of vandalism the local authority threatened to slap a rate and rent demand on Telecom for each box on public land.

A couple of days later The Wizard led a march of 200 people, including a number of bemused tourists, to a box near Cathedral Square and, amid chants, fireworks and heckles, repainted the box red. "Redvolution" was declared.

Telecom finally relented and said it would paint the boxes red again.

Victory may be sweet — and it may be short. The red wooden boxes are destined to make way for new pay phones anyway.

Page 16— Australasian POST, January 21, 1989

The following morning the Red Army was called to the colours and officers of the local regiment of Alf's Imperial Army leapt into action and repainted the only really beautiful phone box in the South Island, the design classic 'K7' in Victoria Square.

I have a brush with the law

Both daily newspapers joined in the fun on Wednesday as Telecom executives began threatening me and Alf's Imperial Army with the dire legal consequences of our persistence.

After one of my daily free speeches in Cathedral Square, the police approached me to warn me that, if I continued with the repainting, I faced a possible fine as high as $150 for vandalism. I observed that I was looking forward to defending myself in a court case in which restoring a phone box to its previous colour was regarded as the same sort of offence as smashing phone box windows, cutting the wires or spraying graffiti.

City council enters the fray

To my delight and surprise, on the same eventful day came a report that Councillor John Burn, head of the inner city working party, was highly supportive of the campaign to bring life and colour to the city. He even said he would bring the matter up at Monday's council meeting in order to propose that the council should provide me and my army with free red paint!

Truce

Late on Wednesday I was informed that Telecom would hold a survey of public opinion on their colour preferences for phone boxes. They would use hundreds of pupils from the two longest-established private schools in the city, Christ's College and St Margaret's, to survey 10,000 people. My army and I declared a truce and promised to cease painting until the results were published in three days' time.

Meanwhile pupils at the Rudolph Steiner School, true to their beliefs in the spiritual importance of colour, conducted their own survey of 385 people. They found only thirteen percent wanted the boxes to be blue and ten percent didn't like or use phone boxes and didn't care what colour they were. The rest were emphatic in their preference for recognisable and traditional red. However Telecom would not accept these results and waited for their own.

Desperately seeking solutions

Desperate Telecom managers brought in a consultant 'colour psychologist' in an attempt to vindicate their choice of pale blue paint. The district manager stated in that he personally believed that red made people angry and caused them to vandalise the phone boxes. Blue, he claimed, would have a soothing effect. Comment continued on national television and in the papers over the weekend.

Telecom admits defeat

The Telecom survey, finally published on 17 October, showed that eighty-eight percent preferred red, six percent preferred blue, one percent yellow, one percent green, and four percent didn't care. Telecom took out a large ad in the local papers to announce the results of the survey and reluctantly admitted defeat but insisted that the eighty or so phone boxes that had been painted blue should remain so until completely new 'safe and functional' pay-phones, which they planned to install the following year, were in place. This was something of a surprise to everyone.

I gave Telecom an ultimatum: either they immediately repaint the blue boxes red, or war would recommence.

City council supplies free ammunition

At their monthly meeting on Monday night, to almost everyone's amazement and delight, the Christchurch City Council decided, by a vote of fifteen to three, that since Telecom was refusing to repaint the blue boxes, they would supply the Wizard and Alf's Imperial Army with free red paint from their stores.

After my customary speech on Wednesday, together with the Red Army and leading my customary crowd of tourists, I marched to the phone box behind the Cathedral. Trumpets were sounded and the repaint was on again. We went through town, painting phone boxes in prominent sites. Cars hooted approval, crowds cheered and clapped the heroes.

But when the Red Army marched smartly into the council's stores to collect the red paint allocated to them by the democratically elected Christchurch City Council they met with ill-concealed hostility and a refusal to supply the paint. Eventually the staff gritted their teeth and gave us one very small pot.

Putting in the boot

On Thursday Councillor Burn warned Telecom that, if they persisted in their arrogant and stupid attitude, he would recommend that the city council should start charging rent for the land the boxes sat on. Then the adjoining Waimairi Council actually passed a resolution to that effect.

The newspapers were full of letters, most of them making fun of Telecom, and the affair grew from the talk of the town to the talk of the world. A Japanese current affairs programme sent a team to New Zealand just to film me painting a phone box. They couldn't believe that any sane man would take on a multinational corporation almost single-handed – and succeed.

Telecom surrenders unconditionally

On Friday 21 October, surrounded on all sides by determined enemies of their 'poofy blue' phone boxes, Telecom caved in. The war, like all successful wars, was short and decisive. It had lasted twelve days.

Magnanimous in victory, as I had been courageous in adversity, I made up with Telecom and accepted 'tribute' of one of the two remaining old-fashioned wooden boxes with a pointed roof, whose friendly light across the road I could see from my bedroom window at my previous residence. This was to be delivered when the new plastic horrors were installed.

Finally, in July 1990, in the presence of the Red Army and myself, the design classic 'K7' iron phone kiosk came back from maintenance and repair and was restored to Victoria Square, where, to this day, it delights the eye of locals and tourists alike.

Catastrophe narrowly averted

In June 1991 an act of cultural barbarism was committed by Telecom when they erected one of their new hideous 'plastic fantastics' right in the middle of the city council's pride and joy, the tastefully redesigned Worcester Boulevard, which runs through the Victorian Gothic Arts Centre.

Convinced that Telecom had learnt a costly lesson in Christchurch, I was surprised to find, during a visit to Invercargill early the following year, half a dozen canary yellow phone boxes. On 16 February, with the help of the 7th Cargill Dragoons of Alf's Imperial Army, I painted the most conspicuous of the offensive objects red again. The same day, six members of the Dunedin Regiment, led by their local wizard, were arrested and charged with malicious damage when they repainted one of the yellow perils in their city.

I was alerted by the manager of the Arts Centre and prepared for action. As soon as Telecom heard that there was a storm brewing they wisely invited me up to the top floor for tea and bikkies with the chiefs. Common sense and mutual respect won the day but Telecom management found that they had sold all their old wooden phone boxes to the public, whose passion for them was insatiable.

They asked me very nicely if I was prepared to donate my 'tribute' (the old phone box they had promised to give me and which was currently being restored) to the people of Christchurch for erection in Worcester Boulevard. I had been dreaming of having the old box, complete with friendly light, in my garden, but I choked back my tears of disappointment and agreed.

A unique memorial

Any visitor to Christchurch who has been touched by this moving finale to a ripping good story may go inside the little old phone box near the tram stop in Worcester Boulevard, and they will find there a commemorative plaque informing the world that the phone box was donated by the Wizard and Telecom to the people of Christchurch.

18
Wizard of New Zealand

The Newman Award

My career was not entirely blighted by the authorities' lack of vision and humour. Bruce Dunstan, the executive officer of the Canterbury Tourism Council, had stood by me and defended me from many bureaucratic attacks. I'm sure he had a lot to do with my getting the prestigious Newman Award for contributions to New Zealand tourism in 1989. He, too, received an award that year for his innovative approach to promoting Canterbury. I felt I had at last come in from the cold.

Confessions of a living work of art

In 1990, for the first time since 1969, I was asked to give a lecture at university. This revolutionary event came about as a result of Alice's tutoring at the Canterbury University School of Fine Arts. We had come to know some of the staff, and Dr Denis Dutton considered that my persistence in preserving my identity as a living work of art was remarkable in its own right and worthy of discussion by his students.

There was a huge turnout as I entered in my usual regalia, smoking a fine cigar given me by Denis, then removed my hat and gown to appear in the costume of a government-funded career intellectual. My lecture, entitled 'Confessions of a Living Work of Art', produced considerable interest. It was like coming home after twenty years of exile.

Emy dies

A few weeks later, after a year of declining health and pain, my mother died, aged eighty-seven. At last the waiting was over for her. She had been pining for her beloved Arthur, who had died so tragically early twenty-seven years before.

Neolithic monuments are frequently decorated with a mysterious

double spiral, winding out from one centre and then changing direction to wind back into another centre. I had made the transition into the new orbit around my thirty-fifth year, and I was deeply grateful that my mother had been one of the few people who had not been horrified at my change of direction.

My mother, Emy, who died in 1990 at the age of eighty-seven, shared my love of a good stir.

I am appointed Wizard of New Zealand

Maybe it was not just chance that, within a few weeks of the death of my last contact with my basic origins, I received a boost to increase my velocity towards my new centre of being. During the brief period in 1990 that Mike Moore was Prime Minister, he bumped into me at the Arts Centre and told me that, if I agreed, he would appoint me official Wizard of New Zealand. Normally fairly reticent, I got very excited and gave him a big hug. I was overjoyed.

The day before the 1990 election I was in Cathedral Square on my ladder pontificating as usual when Mike approached with his entourage. I greeted him and asked if he would like to address the crowd from my ladder. In exchange I requested that, if he won the election, he would do all he could to bring South Up maps into every classroom to give our young people a chance to overcome our national geographical inferiority complex.

He accepted my offer and made his last speech as PM from my ladder. What a proud moment. An American tourist in the crowd was heard to ask. 'Which guy is the Prime Minister? The bald guy or the guy with the pointy hat?' What a moment. Isn't life wonderful?

In 1990, New Zealand's sesquicentennial year, I finally became the first Wizard of New Zealand.

PRIME MINISTER

PROCLAMATION

Be it known by all and singular that the Wizard of Christchurch, Living Work of Art at the National Gallery of Victoria and the Robert MacDougall Art Gallery in Christchurch, and Cosmologer of the University of Melbourne, formerly known as Ian Brackenbury Channell; is hereby appointed the first Wizard of New Zealand, entitled to wear the appropriate regalia and be required to carry out the duties of national Wizard, namely to protect the Government, to bless new enterprises, cast out evil spirits, upset fanatics, cheer up the population, attract tourists and in particular to design and promote a new and improved universe which puts New Zealand on top of the world both physically and metaphysically.

Given under my hand, this Sixth Day of October, in the Year of Our Lord 1990, Sesquicentennial year of the Dominion of New Zealand.

The Right Honourable Mike Moore
Member of Parliament
Prime Minister of New Zealand

Saving the Queen from the Reserve Bank

Suddenly, out of the blue, the appositely named Governor of the Reserve Bank, Don Brash, announced that he thought it was time to remove the Queen's head from our banknotes and replace it with pictures of important New Zealanders. There had been no public demand for this or even discussion. We were outraged. This was treason. The Crown is still the legitimate authority in New Zealand and not 'the people'. Swift decisive action was required.

On 10 June 1991 the wizards in Dunedin, Christchurch and Wellington mobilised the regiments of Alf's Imperial Army. We delivered an ultimatum for the bank to withdraw their treasonable proposals by 14 June or a state of war would exist between us. We received no such assurance, and so, on 15 June, the army marched on the Reserve Bank offices in Wellington, Dunedin and Christchurch. We brought our cannon with us ready to fire upon the Reserve Bank in Hereford Street. Just as we were about to lay siege to the building, an official came out of the bank waving a piece of paper. Was this 'peace in our time'?

Betrayed by bankers

The order was given to hold fire while the branch manger approached me and Lieutenant Stephen Symons (now Town Crier of Christchurch) and stated that the bank had conceded to our demands. In explanation he showed us what turned out to be the prototype of a new $10 banknote. To our surprise and delight it portrayed not only the Queen's head but also my own.

Promised discussion over the Reserve Bank's 'suggestion' never took place. Without public approval the bank went ahead and did what they were going to do anyway. The $20 bill, however, was saved by our timely action and was the only banknote to retain the Queen's head, although my own was missing!

Licensing a wizard

The only licence I held at this time was my Artistic Licence, bound in leather, lettered in gold and signed by John Coley, the director of the McDougall Art Gallery. As a conceptual art form I had driving for twenty years without a driving licence. Of course this meant I had to be pretty careful as a driver. I had never had my licence revoked so it was not a crime against the spirit of the law. The police turned a blind eye so long as I drove carefully.

At this point I must put in a word for the police, who have always co-operated with me to a remarkable degree. It is strange that so many intellectual and religious radicals regard me as some sort of threat whereas the police, and for that matter most people without intellectual pretensions, can see exactly what I am up to, and join in the fun.

There was a groundswell from killjoy members of the public who, hearing my boasts in the Square that I lived on trust and had no documents from the state, insisted I should be like ordinary people and have a proper driving licence. I was perfectly happy to take a driving test but did not want to be

My push-me-pull-you Volkswagen. A few years ago I found a car more suitable than my old Holden station wagon for my school visits and so on – a Volkswagen made from two front ends welded back to back. It took my fancy the first time I set eyes on it in a classic cars saleroom. Since it has identical steering wheels, dashboards, wipers and so on, at each end, I frequently have trouble finding the right door to get in. It has been a great hit with tourists as I park it outside the cathedral while I speak. I found that if one's car is preposterous enough, parking is no problem.

turned back into a legal person. I like being born again.

I passed my test with flying colours. Soon afterwards, when I was helping the traffic police with their campaign against drinking drivers, they presented me with a large scroll in beautiful calligraphy which they informed me was my special Wizard's Driving Licence! The scroll reads as follows: 'Let it be known that The Wizard is duly authorised to operate a horseless carriage in the city of Christchurch and the environs of the land of New Zealand for perpetuity'. If stopped and asked for my licence, all I had to do was show the scroll. Another triumph for my fun revolutionary approach to humanising and re-enchanting the world.

British land rights march, claiming back the Queen's Chain on Banks Peninsula.

19
Alice gets her man

A shocking announcement

To the amazement of the people of New Zealand I announced early in 1992 that I had received a proposal of marriage and was giving it serious consideration. This was a real shock to my regular listeners, who had heard me say repeatedly that a wise man does not marry and that any wizard who does so loses his powers. My male fans felt really let down and my female fans could not conceal their sense of 'I-told-you-so' triumph.

How did this all come about? Our mayor Vicki Buck loved festivals and had the very original idea of a Festival of Romance for Christchurch to be held around Valentine's Day. She had been very kind to me over the years and she told me that she needed something special to provide a highlight for the first festival.

Thinking it over, I decided that, since I owed a lot to Alice, who had been dropping subtle hints about a wedding for the past twenty years or so, I might repay both of them by allowing Alice to get within sight of her goal. I was also forced to admit that my grand plan, to be a master with three or four young female slaves, had proved impossible to achieve, in spite of my inspired efforts.

An agonising decision

National newspapers and television news programmes showed me, torn with doubt, agonising over the decision in the days leading up to the opening ball when I would give my answer. I let no one know the identity of the mystery woman, which added to the suspense and was a great boost to the publicity for the new festival. Of course all our friends had guessed but they kept quiet.

The hour arrived when I was to make my decision. Resplendent in top hat and tails, I stood on the stage and, before the cameras, I announced that my answer was 'Yes'. To the cheers of the crowd, Alice, dressed in a beautiful

gown, was escorted up to the stage by our friend, the Town Crier. I put the ring on her finger, we kissed, Vicki presented us both with baskets of flowers and the Festival of Romance was well and truly opened.

Spiritual impediments

There were a number of difficulties to overcome before we could actually get married. Alice, being a Roman Catholic, regards marriage as one of the sacraments. It is seen by the church as primarily a union concerned with building an economic household and producing offspring. As a postmodern wizard, my view of marriage is more romantic and I see it as a union of opposites brought about through personal alchemy.

Could we find a compromise between these two very different views of marriage? Even marrying a Catholic without being turned into one was difficult enough. Alice has never had any hidden agenda: she is far too honest and romantic to act as a 'fifth columnist'. The church might, however, still consider marrying us in the hope that her mere goodness would eventually triumph over my stubborn apostasy.

In the meantime the then Governor-General, Dame Cath Tizard, confided to Alice in my presence that she was a marriage celebrant and offered her services. Moreover, every chance she got, and especially with a large crowd listening, the mayor kept making hurtful comments about the delay.

The Wizard and Oz

Unlike the Wizard in the book, who was trying to get out of Oz, I was still trying to get in. Now, however, armed with the most unlikely official document in the world, my special Wizard's driving licence from the traffic police, I renewed my efforts. Over the years cabinet ministers in both Labour and National governments had kindly made considerable efforts to find a solution to the passport problem, and we had almost been successful.

I had been invited to go to Melbourne and Sydney to be part of a major travel show and, following pressure from the Canterbury Tourism Council, in May 1992 the Minister of Immigration and the local immigration officer had provided me with a document called a 'Certificate of Identity'. This was ideal for a conceptual art form, and simply named me as 'Wizard of New Zealand'.

The Wizard and Alice, engaged at last.
PETER TOWERS

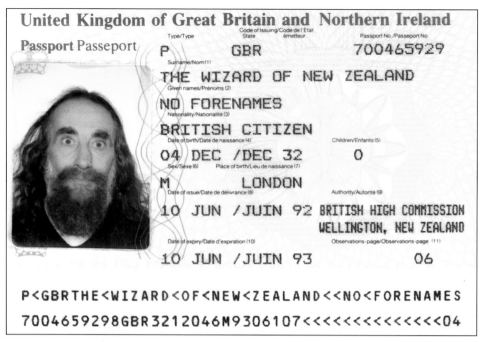

United Kingdom of Great Britain and Northern Ireland

Passport Passeport

Type/Type: **P**
Code of Issuing/Code de l'Etat State émetteur: **GBR**
Passport No./Passeport No: **700465929**

Surname/Nom (1): **THE WIZARD OF NEW ZEALAND**

Given names/Prénoms (2): **NO FORENAMES**

Nationality/Nationalité (3): **BRITISH CITIZEN**

Date of birth/Date de naissance (4): **04 DEC /DEC 32**
Children/Enfants (5): **0**

Sex/Sexe (6): **M**
Place of birth/Lieu de naissance (7): **LONDON**

Date of issue/Date de délivrance (8): **10 JUN /JUIN 92**
Authority/Autorité (9): **BRITISH HIGH COMMISSION WELLINGTON, NEW ZEALAND**

Date of expiry/Date d'expiration (10): **10 JUN /JUIN 93**
Observations-page/Observations-page (11): **06**

P<GBRTHE<WIZARD<OF<NEW<ZEALAND<<NO<FORENAMES
7004659298GBR3212046M9306107<<<<<<<<<<<<<<04

My Wizard of New Zealand passport, issued in 1992.

The Australian government panics

I was all set to go when, a few days before the show was due to open, there was an almighty eruption from the Minister of Immigration in Australia. Even though the document was a perfectly legal one as far as the New Zealand government was concerned, he would not have a bar of it, on the basis of an obscure technicality.

I had to act quickly and decisively. Aussie Malcolm, the Minister of Immigration who had been so helpful ten years earlier and had been appointed 'wizard third class' for his efforts, had set up a successful immigration advice service. He set his talented staff on to the problem. A member of the British High Commission staff (praise be to this wonderful lady) found an obscure regulation that enabled the High Commissioner to issue me a British passport within twenty-four hours made out to 'The Wizard of New Zealand' (no other names). We had beaten the bastards. Aussie couldn't believe it, and nor could I. It was like a passport for the Tooth Fairy or Father Christmas!

Just in time

Off I went to arrive in Melbourne a few minutes before the opening. I was in too much of a hurry to really appreciate the feeling of freedom. I was able to leave New Zealand and return at will. At Melbourne Airport the customs and immigration officials were so amazed at my passport, no doubt enhanced by my travelling outfit of black pointy hat and gown, that they politely asked me if they could photocopy it!

Coming out of customs, I spied two more black pointy hats and gowns in the crowd. Wizards Charlie Ferrari and David Greagg were there to welcome me. It was only a short trip but it was wonderful to be back in Oz, where it had all begun. I was able to be part of a sister-city visit to Adelaide the next year with the mayor, councillors and business entrepreneurs.

I return to my roots in England

Alice had been working hard at teaching and we had some money to spend for a change so off we went to London on a cheap fare. We were met at Heathrow by a driver provided by my sister. He whisked us into London to her balloon-bedecked Georgian terrace house near St Pancras Station, which was to be our base.

It was a wonderful holiday. I was able to show Alice the places where I used to live in Suffolk, South London, Notting Hill and Leeds. We were most keen to visit the cathedrals, country houses and castles, but only scratched the surface in the month we were there together. Of course I travelled incognito. It was my turn to be a tourist.

A high point was a special gathering of the Brackenbury clan in an ancient pub. My Uncle Jack, now in his eighties, could still act the fool with considerable élan. I had come back to my roots in every way.

The last thing I did before returning home to Christchurch was to go to London's famous Hyde Park Corner on a Sunday. The other orators were nearly all serious one-issue obsessives and did not compare with me for either verbosity or passion. Soon after I began speaking in my wizard outfit I was spotted by quite a number of New Zealand tourists. They became very excited and informed the incredulous crowd that I was really was a wizard back home. They were swollen with pride at having such a remarkable man as a fellow Kiwi.

I sacrifice my beard for the Labour Party

My extraordinary powers lay partly in my hair, which barbers' scissors have not touched since 1968. The Bible, folklore and anthropological studies all agree on the importance of realising this. Oaths are even sworn on the beards of prophets.

The Labour Party had recently split into two, with Jim Anderton leading a breakaway group of old-fashioned socialists, strangely named New Labour. I was concerned that New Zealand was going lose the most important ingredient of a democratic government – two equally strong parties in and out of power. While the split lasted how could two weak Labour parties ever keep the National government on its toes?

I felt I owed one to Mike Moore for appointing me Wizard of New Zealand, so I decided to make a real sacrifice. I was prepared to mutilate my image and lose some of my precious hair by shaving off my beard. The Labour Party had mutilated itself and could heal itself, just as my beard could grow again.

On the appointed day, in December 1993, surrounded by the media, I sat outside the cathedral and began the process of destroying the thirty-five-year-old beard of the prophet. The news of my self-mutilation travelled round the world and featured prominently in the *Kathmandu Post* in the overseas news section, next to a story about Mother Theresa!

Alas, my sacrifice was in vain and did not bring about a reconciliation between Mike and Jim and their colleagues. It was all rather a waste of time because a few years later the foolish Kiwis voted for MMP.

I did not recognise myself. It had been a long time since I last saw myself. I did not like the look of me and would not have bought a used car from a man with a face like that. Alice was shocked and in tears. This was not the man she fallen in love with. What could I do? I got some theatrical glue and stuck the whiskers on again. I looked rather scruffy, but that was nothing new.

20

The rain-dance kid

A city in trouble

The 1994 water crisis in Auckland was so grave that no baths were allowed and toilets were flushed only when absolutely necessary. Watercare Services approached me to do a rain dance for them. Loath to intrude on other people's territory without being invited by the legitimate authorities, I asked them to arrange an invitation from one or more of the four city councils that administer Auckland.

Only North Shore showed any interest. I received a delightful letter of invitation (with a charming little poem), looking forward to my visit and informing me that many children would love to be present. The date was set for late May, unless, of course, it rained before then.

Not my first experience

This was not my first experience of rain dancing. In the summer of the wonderful year of 1988, which had seen the Telephone Box War, I had received a request from the small South Canterbury town of Waimate to attend their annual Agricultural and Pastoral Show with the aim of doing something to break their six-month drought. Inspired by the old Hollywood film *The Rainmaker*, I decided it could do no harm, and would certainly cheer up the depressed locals, to try out my skill as a rainmaker. I accepted the challenge and said I would design a special rain dance for the occasion.

Satanic forces

As soon as the local Assembly of God heard that a wizard was coming to do a rain dance they were enraged and demanded that the invitation be rescinded. They put pressure on the mayor and council and said they would withdraw financial support from the show.

A battle between the forces of Good and Evil broke out. The mayor and show committee wouldn't back down and the media, who thrive on such things, made a big issue out of it. When I arrived in Waimate some weeks later it still hadn't rained and the local population and a curious TVNZ crew were abuzz with anticipation.

Slowly I assembled my rain-making equipment, which included four buckets of water, a horn, an umbrella under which hung a small red demon, a large bass drum, my magic staff and a mug of beer. No sooner had I begun my circular gyrations, while beating my drum, than a strange black cloud, more like smoke than water vapour, appeared over Waimate. An hour or two later, torrential rain began to fall and the show was washed out. The downpour, which continued all night, fell mainly in the Waimate valley and bypassed other regions.

I adjourned to the refreshment tent to watch the downpour and partake of the free whiskies that were thrust into my hands by visibly shaken farmers. The weatherman on the national TV news that night began his description of the weather with: 'You're not going to believe this, but . . .'

Waimate's fame reaches New York

A day or two later a whole page of the *New York Times* was devoted to me and my spectacularly successful rain dance. This was the first time the name of the town of Waimate had been trumpeted abroad.

I don't accept payment for weather magic, expecting only the recognition due to my courage in undertaking such a risky business, where failure means much mockery from believers in both God and Nature. On this occasion it occurred to me that the district could show its gratitude and at the same time solve its major economic problem of being off the main north–south highway and being by-passed by all the tourist buses. I wrote to the mayor, requesting that the town should construct a memorial 'shrine' at the site and put up a signpost at the highway turn-off bearing the words 'Wizard's Shrine 3 Miles'.

My colleague the Wizard of Dunedin, being a sculptor, was prepared to execute a bronze memorial in the form of a combined drinking-fountain and horse trough. Water would descend through bronze clouds on to the figure of a drum-beating and dancing wizard and then drain into the trough below. Under the figure, in Latin of course, would be the inscription, 'TRUST ME: I KNOW WHAT I'M DOING'. Japanese tour buses would thunder into Waimate, bringing a thriving trade in rain-dance memorabilia and older residents could entertain visitors with eye-witness accounts and would never need to buy their own drinks during the tourist season.

A wet Wizard in Waimate.

Alas, the request met with bitter opposition from my main rivals, the churches in Waimate, even though it was obvious that God must love me more than them since He had withheld the rain in spite of their prayers and sent it when I danced. Unless, of course, the rain was 'satanic', in which case the farmers shouldn't have taken advantage of it.

In 1989, at the invitation of the local radio station and the mayor, who also put me up at his house, I performed another rain dance in Nelson, which had a critical water shortage, and a few days later it rained heavily, very heavily, and continuously. On a visit there a few months later I received many complaints.

Auckland, a city ruled by fear

In 1994, a day or two before my departure for Auckland, like a thunderbolt out of the blue, I received a letter from North Shore regretting that they had to cancel their invitation as they had been deluged, not with rain, but by a massive number of complaints that, since I was a practitioner of the black arts, I should under no circumstances be allowed to come.

The talkback radio stations were dominated for several days by a very serious debate as to whether the Wizard should be allowed to go north. Everyone outside Auckland was amazed and justifiably alarmed at the revelation that the city was being influenced and even controlled by a very powerful and influential group of religious maniacs.

A Yankee wizard to the rescue

Then a fax arrived from an unknown wizard in a small town just north of Auckland, offering to help in winning the spiritual war that was raging there. Wizard Ron was an American living in Silverdale and was on good terms with the district mayor and local businessmen's association.

The mayor of the Rodney District sent the invitation and, in a blaze of media publicity, I arrived on 7 July to dance in the main street of tiny Silverdale, assisted by my new Yankee colleague. The place was packed and, to my great delight, I observed that lots of the children present were wearing little pointy hats.

A spell from the sky

To ensure success, a helicopter was chartered to fly me over Auckland city while I made suitable gestures and chants to encourage precipitation. At the same time my voice was broadcast over a local radio station. I urged the population down below to look up and, when they saw my plane, to demonstrate their support by doing a few dance steps, or their disapproval by shaking their fists.

Three days after my rain dance, and without warning, the rains came. And came. And came. It rained heavily in Auckland for three years. In spite of receiving a large number of private letters politely requesting me to return to Auckland to stop the rain, I made it quite clear that, since none of the councils would write to thank me for saving them from a serious crisis, I would just let the rain continue unabated.

Australia calls for help

This incredible story does not end here. The final (?) chapter took place a few weeks after I won the battle over the souls of Auckland. I received a phone call from radio station 2GB in Sydney begging my assistance to break the catastrophic seven-year drought in the outback of New South Wales and Queensland. I decided to try my 'luck' just one more time and once again insisted that it be at the invitation of a city or district council. Tamworth in New South Wales invited me to perform my legendary rain dance in their region.

The media attention waiting for me on arrival in Sydney was hard to believe, though the general mood was, to put it mildly, one of extreme scepticism. I announced that, should my rain dance break the drought, the only reward I sought was the title of 'Wizard of Australia'. As I was already the official Wizard of New Zealand I wished to combine the titles to become 'Wizard of Australasia'.

The Sydney Opera House, plus lurking Wizard.

After a warm welcome in Tamworth and a good lunch I proceeded to a parched paddock under a sun blazing in a clear blue sky. Present was a small gathering of bankrupt farmers and Aboriginal tribal elders I had invited through my extensive network of friendly nuns. With me was a TV3 camera crew who had come across the Tasman to film the whole episode. I performed the rain dance once again on rock-hard ground.

My mission completed, I returned exhausted to Sydney and was preparing to pack and leave for New Zealand when the news came through that huge storm clouds were gathering over Tamworth and that thunder and lightning were alarming the locals.

Another miracle

Back in Christchurch I found the TV news programmes were reporting excitedly on heavy rainfalls in the stricken regions, including Tamworth. Film broadcast in New Zealand showed the rain and interviews with the locals, surprisingly few of whom would openly admit that my rain dance had produced the long-awaited rain.

The New Zealanders knew all right and they were filled with pride in the powers of their amazing wizard. Dr Denis Dutton, spokesman for the New Zealand Skeptics, who had unmasked many new-age rip-offs, stated

on national TV that I was the only individual they had ever come across who possesses genuine 'paranormal' powers.

Needless to say, in spite of my achieving the impossible, the Australian government did not make the appointment I sought. I was particularly irked when, shortly afterwards, a coastal shower, so common in Sydney, which occurred during the Pope's visit to beatify the Blessed Mary McKillop, was taken by many as a true miracle and a sign that she was a genuine saint.

On the positive side, being a primitive 'throwback' myself, I'm still chuckling about what must have been said in the powerful oral Aboriginal tribal network about an ex-academic Anglo-Saxon wizard from New Zealand performing a rain dance right before the eyes of their representatives on the prestigious Native Land Rights Council.

I perform my successful rain dance at Tamworth, New South Wales, in November 1994.
NORTHERN LEADER

21
The Log o' Wood returns

For some years nothing particularly unusual happened in my spell-casting for sporting teams. I lost a few, but I won more than I lost. Then in 1994, after ten fairly uneventful years, Canterbury once again captured the Ranfurly Shield and rugby fever gripped Christchurch.

The first major challenge was from our bitter rival Otago, who were now high up in the tables and expected an easy victory. A vast number of their supporters came to Christchurch to make it the best attended provincial rugby game within living memory.

An innovation that proved both dramatic and successful was the pre-match blessing of the Canterbury team's new underpants outside the cathedral. On the day of the great match the Lancaster Park authorities arranged that I should arrive by helicopter to land in the centre of the ground, bringing the Ranfurly Shield to the field of play. Running a bit late, and tightly gripping the precious trophy, I was driven to the airport, with siren screaming, by a kindly policeman. On landing at the packed ground, I blessed the shield to protect it from being taken from us.

Then, with 30,000 eyes on me, I took up my position on the sidelines, using my new red-and-black wand. I was very nervous, though I hoped it didn't show. I had every reason to be apprehensive. It was a cliff-hanger. Canterbury was well down in the first half. In the second half, with my help, they clawed their way back but were still a point down and in the last few minutes of the match they were heading for the Otago touchline. The crowd was delirious.

At the last moment, the Otago captain intercepted the ball close to where I was standing. It looked as though only a miracle could save Canterbury. I conjured furiously and, to the amazement of the crowd, the referee awarded the home team a penalty. Andrew Mehrtens calmly kicked the goal. The final whistle blew. The crowd went berserk. I was the hero of the hour.

As this photo records, my second-half spell at the Ranfurly Shield game between Canterbury and Otago, was an impressive sight.

No Cantabrian will ever forget that wonderful winter of provincial rugby at its very best. The weather held up. The crowds at Lancaster Park were enormous and the local team played like gods.

Following on my 1994 triumph I was invited by the Rugby Union authorities at Lancaster Park to provide magic for the major challenges in the 1995 season. A band of priestly figures carried banners bearing arcane symbols to back up my incantations, and I also called on the enthusiastic Captain Cordite of Alf's Imperial Army to fire a round each time Canterbury scored a try. Before each match we would process around the field of play with a smoking cauldron before taking up a position near the opponents' goal line with the aim of drawing the ball towards us.

We defended the 'Log o' Wood' from all comers. Waikato, Southland and Wellington, who were all top teams, could not break the magic spell over our players.

A wizard falls from the sky

September 1995 was the 21st anniversary of my arrival in Christchurch and, with the enthusiastic support of the mayor and administrative help from the city council, a special 'Wizard's Week' was organised to celebrate the occasion. Several overseas wizards in town. Destiny conspired that the greatest challenger of all, Auckland, would play Canterbury on the final day of the week.

This was to be my finest hour. All seven wizards would combine their powers at the match and Captain Cordite would bring his tank for extra firepower. Moments before the match started I appeared in the sky over Lancaster Park and slowly descended by parachute, while uttering anathemata against the Auckland team. With the cauldron smoking, we wizards conjured up a great victory spell to end the season.

Cursed!

Slowly it dawned on us that something was amiss. Our team were not playing their usual fast and daring game. They were stricken with terror as if they were being attacked by demons. The Auckland team were menacing and humourless and simply stomped on their opponents.

The tank was not called on to fire a single round. In spite of the combined efforts of the wizards and their banner-bearing priestly attendants, the Canterbury team was obliterated by 30–0. I had a terrible feeling of *déjà vu*.

The crowd was shocked. We were even more shocked. Then we realised what had happened. Two days before, while all the wizards were busy performing a ritual, a pair of fundamentalist fanatics from the New Life Centre had grabbed our magic staffs and taken them into the Anglican cathedral for a desecration ceremony. Unlike witches, most wizards are supporters of orthodox religion, and we regarded the incident as malevolent and insulting to the church that had founded the city of Christchurch. And the ceremony had worked. We simply could not imagine individuals so depraved that they could hate wizards, Anglicans and rugby!

Realising that the loss of the shield to Auckland was not our fault and that powerful forces of evil had been unleashed, we hurriedly wrapped our contaminated staffs in pure woollen material and put them away until the evil enchantment had worn off.

I was spared from the sackcloth and ashes again, but to date I have not been asked to cast any more spells for the Canterbury rugby team.

22

Wizards' Day of Rage

The hatching

As part of my Wizard's Week, held in September 1995, I hatched out of a giant egg in the Robert McDougall Art Gallery. Before the hatching, visiting wizards from all parts of New Zealand, and Charlie and David from Melbourne, had circled round the egg, constructed by Wayne the Dunedin wizard, doing the wizard 'hum', a kind of conflation of a Buddhist chant and a Pooh hum. The hatching was conducted with the assistance of cultural midwives in masks and gowns – the mayor, Mike Moore, the assistant director of the gallery and so on. Meanwhile, Kinder Surprise eggs were presented to all the official guests.

The egg, in the centre of the beautiful marble atrium of the Robert McDougall Art Gallery, was surrounded by the Living Work of Art Exhibition. The exhibition itself, curated by Alice, was made up of mounted press cuttings and historical photos of important events in my life.

Wizards' nest

With the help of the School of Fine Arts of Canterbury University and the sculpture students, under the kind direction of Fiona Gunn, a large wizards' nest was built high up on top of the university library tower. Modelled on a stork's nest, it was an ideal place for wizards to gather and meditate.

The visiting wizards were in Christchurch for the anniversary but also to attend a wizards' conclave. They were all dressed in identical black gowns and pointy hats and were almost indistinguishable, which gave rise to many confusions of identity.

These fish-eye views show the egg in the atrium of the Robert McDougall Gallery and the beautiful polyptych celebrating my twenty-one years in Christchurch.

Left: Six wizards carry the egg down Worcester Boulevard. Right: In the Square, wizards explode from the egg. Below: The Wizards' Nest is destroyed.

158

The stolen image

There's not enough space to go into the full story here but a row had been brewing between me and the Mount Cook group. They had used my image as the major element in a publicity campaign without my knowledge or permission and without making any payment. Lawyers told me that the typical rate for the use of anyone's image in such a major campaign, involving full-page advertisements in major newspapers, posters and T-shirts was around five percent of the advertising budget. Judging by the number of ads in the major Sydney papers, we estimated this must have been something like $500,000. Since the Mount Cook Group management was acting so short-sightedly, and illegally, and had not responded to polite letters from our solicitor, the best thing to do was to send them a bill for $25,000. Of course the money would have to go to Alice since, as a living work of art and postmodern prophet, I still have no bank accounts or property. Any delay in payment would simply add interest to the debt they owed me.

This was duly done. There was no reply. It was time for direct action.

Wizards' Day of Rage

Since all the wizards were in town, we decided to hold a Day of Rage. Accompanied by our friendly 'monks' carrying banners reading 'Mt Cook Exploits Wizards', six wizards carried the giant egg with a hole in it, from which I had earlier hatched, down the 'sacred way' of Christchurch, Worcester Boulevard, which links the cultural centre to the social centre, Cathedral Square.

After almost an hour of wizard 'hums' around our smoking cauldron and processing around the Square, all seven wizards entered the egg. There was much muffled angry chanting and the egg began to shake, rattle and roll ominously. There was a loud explosion and lots of smoke and the egg split open like a ripe fruit, spilling out angry wizards in all directions, narrowly missing the TV personnel covering the event. We then picked up the chunks of egg and began to break them over each other's heads. It was an awesome sight and the large crowd watched in amazement. Finally we threw the pieces of egg to the people, assuring them that these possessed magical healing properties.

The wizards then raced over to the University Library and, temporarily breaking the concentration of students studying for their finals, took the lift to the top floor, rushed over to the huge nest and, in a paroxysm of rage, tore it apart with their bare hands.

Their last act was to go their hotel room where a local Internet pioneer and wizard enthusiast, Mark Stevens, had prepared a computer terminal. They all gathered round and, after a suitable 'hum' and a few incantations, I pressed a key to send a message around the web at the speed of light: 'The Wizard is Coming'.

In the weeks that followed, the apprentice wizards in Christchurch cast spells on the Mount Cook Group headquarters in Riccarton. The first involved the firing of tiny wizards across Riccarton Road from our cannon. Each carried the name and powers of one of the wizards' conclave. The second spell involved anathemata cast by a wizard circle. As each uttered the powerful words his pointy hat exploded. This last dramatic spell was filmed and later shown by *Eurotrash*, the sensational British TV programme, which had sent a team to New Zealand just to film me. The curses were extremely successful as the coach line began to fail shortly afterwards, and in three years was no more.

The Wizard in cyberspace

Part of my Day of Rage had been to launch myself into cyberspace. This proved a most exciting development.

Forty-nine wizards converged on Christchurch when I launched my website.

PRESS

The weather for Wizards' Week was splendid. In full regalia, including their imposing, if somewhat impractical, hats, the wizards went to sample the outdoor attractions of the region. Those who saw them packed into a jet boat, shooting past the camera on the local TV news, are unlikely to forget it. They went hot-air ballooning and took a trip up the Gondola for a conclave meeting. A particularly happy day was spent paddling in the sea at Sumner and, of course, making a giant sandcastle and performing elaborate rituals around it. Here, left to right, Wizard David of Melbourne, me, Wizard Ron of Silverdale, Wizard Charlie of Melbourne, and Wizards Tony and Phil, both of Wellington.

For twenty-five years I had been marginalised and trivialised by my enemies and Cathedral Square had been the only place I could communicate the good news of the coming of the Fun Revolution and the end of female control after eight thousand years of male bondage. Now I could break out through the Internet where no one could trivialise or censor my ideas. I could reveal all at last. Hooray!

The final event of Wizards' Week was the memorable Wizards' Disco. Strobe lights illuminated the dancing wizards; it was an eerie sight. There was only the unfortunate incident with the Ranfurly Shield match to mar a perfect Wizards' Week. All the wizards went home tired but happy. The modern world does not much like wizards, and they rarely get a chance for a get-together, so this had been really special.

161

Logic, love and levity

The ideal event with which to conclude this story of my life took place on the winter solstice in 1997. Forty-nine wizards came out of the time tunnel on top of Mount Cavendish bearing white tablets carrying a message for the world. In twos and threes, they came down in gondola cars and waited below for me to emerge and descend like Moses with tablets bearing the complete message.

As I descended in the open service car, I blew my magic horn and held the tablets aloft as the wizards down below raised their arms in salutation. We then proceeded by bus to Cathedral Square where the fundamentalists went spare at the spectacle of a swirling mass of wizards around them, like Muslims around the Black Stone in Mecca.

Finally the wizards marched on the council chambers to present a petition that a special marker stone of the correct magical dimensions bearing the message should be set on the hallowed spot in the Square where I had preached the good news for the past twenty-one years.

What was this most important message? It was my home page on the Internet: **www.wizard.gen.nz**. The new age would combine logic of the Greek natural philosophers, love from the universal Christian church and levity from the British tradition of humour.

Where will it all end? My life has constantly surprised me so far. It may not be a miracle, as the title suggests (publishers, not authors chose titles), but it has been both funny 'ha ha' and funny 'peculiar'.

The ultimate Wizard photo.

CANTERBURY BREWERIES

162

appendix

My highly controversial and unpopular theory about male-female relationships

The hand that rocks the cradle

The paradigm case for all social control and conditioning in the animal kingdom is the mother/offspring relationship. Without being subjected to the power and authority of the mother, offspring would be utterly ill equipped to relate to the outside world. Every infant, including the human child, experiences this relationship. The human male child, dependent on his mother for many years longer than any other animal, is particularly affected. Since his 'master' is of the opposite sex, this may mark him so fundamentally that he may relate to all other women as either goddesses or devils for the rest of his life.

Women are not like any other female animals

The human female differs fundamentally from other female animals in two important points. First, she is always on heat; second, in those cultures that tolerate romance and sensuality in females rather than restricting them to motherly virtues, women have shown they are capable of abandoning themselves and experiencing strong sexual orgasms. No other female animal has this characteristic.

Different male and female bondings

There is evidence in ethology that the human female may bond to a male more strongly than to her children. This also makes her unique. Males do not appear to bond as strongly to a female partner unless they are in fear or awe of her as a mother figure. They tend to bond more strongly with groups of males, though the bond has no sexual component.

Moreover, the source of the discord between men and women is that

Away with the fairies.

men are generally polygamous by instinct (not promiscuous), and women are generally monogamous. The trouble comes when women 'project' on to men their own instinctual monogamy and judge men as monsters for not being the same.

Fatherhood

By becoming a father the man receives 'maternal' compensation for losing control over his own polygamous instincts. By becoming a kind of sacred cow or earth mother, the woman receives 'ego' compensation for her sexual self-denial. Both sexes are given status rewards for obedience to these denial values by their religious or other moral leaders.

The mother/child paradigm a model to copy

The mother/child paradigm, which was the basis for socialisation, can be seen as a model for a 'master/slave' paradigm. Lest the reader jump to conclusions, let me emphasise the importance of the woman making the choice to become the 'slave' of the man to whom she is attracted.

I cannot find a better word than 'slave' (and its reciprocal 'master') to describe a relationship not based on providing food, shelter and other material support, which only children should require. After all, there have been, and still are, so many types of slavery, from the crude complete ownership of war captives, to various forms of bondage and apprenticeship, to subtler forms such as wage slavery, religious devotion to cult leaders or political commitment to charismatic dictators.

None of these, except apprenticeship, has ever appealed to me, but I regard the self-denial and abandonment of romantic passion as both exciting and mystical. The nuns exemplify this best. Personally, I have never felt that romantic love is for the male, as it is essentially regressive to the mother/son relationship and easily becomes immature and destructive of the community as a whole. My new enterprise is to launch the idea of romantic love for women of independent means.

Advantages and disadvantages

The advantage for the man as master is that he is no longer under the emotional control of the woman, backed up by a dysfunctional values system. The disadvantage is that he cannot abandon his slave any more than a mother can abandon her child. He is also held accountable for her mental and spiritual, if not material, wellbeing. The advantage for the woman is that she can leave the relationship if she cannot handle it, without emotional blackmail from the man who, as master, is not dependent on her emotional support.

In so many relationships, neither party is held accountable and they easily spiral out of control. In some others, although the woman holds to the all-pervasive ideology of equality when it suits her, when it doesn't she plays the 'victim' card to bring the man under her manipulative control. Sometimes the man starts out as strong and independent and then begins to collapse into the role of a little boy who needs his mother to look after him and to forgive him, provided he truly repents.

The only stable relationships I see around me are those old-fashioned ones where the woman is strong and the man her frightened but adoring slave. These, however, are dysfunctional for the community as a whole, as the aims of the controlling wives are essentially materialistic.

Fixation on monogamy

I remain puzzled by the current obsession with monogamous marriage, even though so many of these become 'serial monogamy' where the husband or wife (or both) exchanges their current spouse for a new one, with disastrous consequences for any children. Divorce and remarriage are being smiled upon.

But whenever I bring up the subject of polygamous marriage for those who want it, most women's eyes harden and most men giggle at the thought of the sexual variety it offers. They miss my point entirely.

Overleaf: On my home patch in Cathedral Square, Christchurch.
P. MORATH